BROKEN PROMISES
AND LIES
OF THE REPUBLICANS

GENE P. ABEL

Printed in the United States of America.

979-8-88945-126-6 (Paperback)
979-8-88945-127-3 (eBook)

Brilliant Books Literary
137 Forest Park Lane Thomasville
North Carolina 27360 USA

CONTENTS

ACKNOWLEDGEMENT

My sincere thanks to my long-time friend the late Alvin Elliott Rittenhouse Jr. for his encouragement to bring the facts to the voters of our country.

DEDICATION

To our Founding Fathers and the VOTE they
gave us to protect our Republic.
Every American, who cares about our country,
must vote in EVERY election.

1956 REPUBLICAN PARTY PLATFORM

*ASSISTANCE TO LOW-INCOME COMMUNITIES

*PROTECT SOCIAL SECURITY

*PROVIDE ASYLUM TO REFUGEES

*EXTEND MINIMUM WAGE

*IMPROVE UNEMPLOYMENT BENEFITS TO COVER MORE PEOPLE

*STRENGTHEN LABOR LAWS SO WORKERS CAN JOIN UNIONS

*EQUAL PAY REGARDLESS OF SEX

GRITPOST

DEDICATED TO:

Return the GOP to what it stood for in 1956. Prevent the GOP from controlling the White House, House of Representatives and Senate to prevent them from implementing their ideas of "Small government and less spending". These two policies will not solve the major issues we face in America in 2023 and beyond such as:

Global Warming.

    Rebuilding the Infrastructure.
    Balance the budget and pay down the National Debt.
    Fully Fund Social Security so the promises made can be kept.
    Provide comprehensive solution to Immigration.
    Help students pay down the $1.7 Trillion dollars of Student Debt.
    Provide for our National Defense given the dangers from Russia, Chine, North Korea and Iran.
    Healthcare for all Americans that is affordable.

Every one of the above issues cannot be accomplished by "Small Government" or by "Spending cuts". We need "Big Government and increased spending" paid for by returning tax rates to pre 1981 levels for anyone making over $400,000 per year. We must end tax loopholes that allow the very wealthy to avoid paying their taxes and through stricter enforcement of our tax laws.

Prevent the GOP from ever increasing the National Debt like they did from 2017 to 2020 by $7.8 Trillion. This was the largest increase in the Debt during a four year period in our history. THIS FROM THE PARTY THAT WANTS, "SMALL GOVERNMENT AND LESS SPENDING"

PREFACE

T his book was written to inform the reader about two crucial issues affecting us today. First is the failure of the Conservative Agenda to keep the promises made to help improve the lives of low and middle income Americans. The facts documenting this failure were taken from non-political sources that clearly show the results of what happened since 1981 when Ronald Reagan convinced the American People to adopt the Conservative Agenda. Cutting taxes that almost totally go to the wealthy, creating a huge National Debt and ending regulations that endanger our economic system.

The second issue is the **CLEAR AND PRESENT DANGER to our Democracy and Republic from Donald J. Trump and the Republican Party supporting his actions.**

The most important part of my book is Section 7—Summary. If you choose to skim over some of the many Facts and Historical details contained in my book, PLEASE read and reread Section 7! Time is running out to protect the United States of America from the dangers of Donald J. Trump and the Republican Party.

Voters in November 2020, temporarily paused the danger of Donald Trump and the Republicans. The reality is the battle for the sole of America is not over. So long as trump seeks power and Republicans enable him, our Republic is in Jeopardy. This book documents the nature of the risks facing us and show anyone who cares about our future why we cannot allow Donald Trump or the Republicans to regain power. Not in November 2024, not ever!

CHAPTER 1

WHAT IS CONSERVATISM?

I n a nutshell, conservatism is the idea that government should be minimal with the maximum flexibility for the individual and business to operate without interference. This concept limits regulation, control, oversight and taxation.

Some of these concepts embodied in the conservative agenda can be seen in the golden age of the 19th century when a hand full of wealthy financiers and businesspersons all but controlled the economy of the United States. An almost total lack of regulation and control enabled a handful of men such as Cornelius Vanderbilt, Andrew Carnegie, Jay Gould, Pierpont Morgan, and John D. Rockefeller to control the United States.

It was at that point that the term "Robber Barons' or the "Captains of Industry" came into vogue. It became clear to President Teddy Roosevelt that the consequences of allowing this small group of powerful and wealthy individuals to do as they pleased would have an adverse impact on the country at large and control the lives of the vast majority of Americans.

http://en.wikipedia.org/wiki/File:Jdr-king.JPG

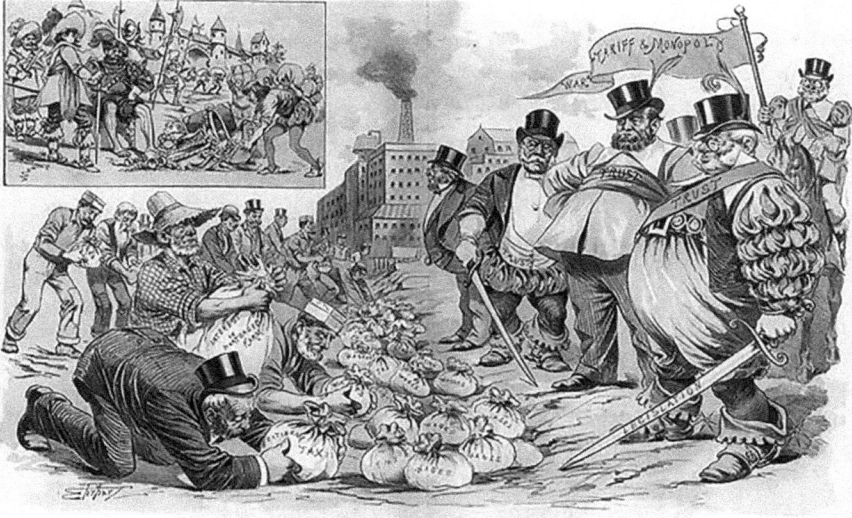

"Opulence in the Gilded Age, 1890," Eyewitness to
History, www.eyewitnesstohistory.com (2008). http://
www.eyewitnesstohistory.com/gildedage.htm

What the robber barons effectively did was purchase power and
directed untold amounts of wealth into their pockets by funding
friendly politicians to enact legislation that would lower taxes, provide
special tax exemptions, prevent anti-trust regulation and establish tax
loopholes that enabled them to accumulate even more wealth. The
impact of this was to enhance the wealth of the few at the expense of
the many. Teddy Roosevelt came into a conflict with the very wealthy
Republicans who supported William Taft. Although Roosevelt was
able to limit many of the abuses that were taking place at the turn-of-
the-century Republicans continued to solidify their connections with
large corporations during the presidencies of Coolidge and Hoover. It
would be difficult to identify a conservative Republican who embraces
Terry Roosevelt as a Republican. He was more like a progressive and
was willing to stand up and confront the impending danger rather than
simply allow these wealthy individuals to operate as they pleased.

The Political Janus. Offset photomechanical print
by Frank A. Nankivell, November 9, 1910.
http://hdl.loc.gov/loc.pnp/ppmsca.27682 http://www.
loc.gov/ pictures/resource/ppmsca.27682/

Although much of the danger that was seen by Teddy Roosevelt with the Captains of Industry was real, it should also be understood that these individuals did produce basic services and industries upon which the economy of the United States was depended for development up until this day. There is no question that these men were ruthless. They drove many into bankruptcy by their misuse of power. Labor was treated like slaves during the construction of the transcontinental railroad. In that respect, some of the negative impacts of the robber barons were similar to the Robber Barons in the 1500's, which is where this term originated. However, because of the lasting impact on the development of our economy and industrial base, they are not all negative by any means.

In addition, at the end of their lives these so-called robber barons used their enormous wealth to fund some of the largest examples of philanthropy the world has ever seen such as The Carnegie Institute and the Rockefeller Foundation. Asa Packer who was a coal magnet did much to help found Lehigh University. Therefore, to be fair to these robber barons yes, they were ruthless and they did cause a lot of harm too many people as they moved forward to develop their enormous power and wealth. However, what they created was of significant benefit to our country as a whole and to our population both during and after their lives. Their enormous contribution to the development and welfare of our country should not be ignored while understanding the dangers posed by their concentration of wealth and power.

Compare and contrast these robber barons with their counterparts today who are using the same tactics to accumulate huge wealth but are not creating anything like the substantive worth that we saw from Carnegie, Packer, and Rockefeller etc. Today we have these conservative billionaires manipulating markets creating unsound mortgages to feather their nests. We see the Hunt brothers manipulating the silver industry not to build or create anything of value except to them. One of the most egregious misuses of power coupled with political intervention was a Credit Default Swap in the mortgage collapse that came to a head September 2008.

Credit Default Swaps were developed by a bunch of Individuals who hired mathematicians to develop schemes simply to create profit for themselves with absolutely no redeeming feature whatsoever. At the time these credit default swaps (CDS) came into being and were used to prop up the bad mortgages, not one person in a million understood what they were or their purpose. However, the people who develop the CDS and the politicians that protected them understood. As companies like Countrywide were busy creating designer loans that were unsound from the outset, other people decided to sell these Ponzi schemes known as credit default swaps.

The pitch was a fee a credit default swap would make a bank or the holder of a bad mortgage whole for any mortgages that went into default. These instruments were written very carefully to avoid being legally termed insurance so they would not run into the entanglement of any state insurance laws or commissions.

In September 2000, Senator Phil Gramm(R-TX), the Chair of the Senate Banking Committee, was quoted as insisting that any bill brought to the Senate floor would need to be expanded to include prohibitions on SEC regulation of the credit default swaps. In December 2000, it is believed that Sen. Gramm added a provision to an omnibus spending bill that prevented Congress from controlling or having oversight into the sale of credit default swaps. In essence, the federal government was used to provide a guard all shield for those selling these worthless Ponzi schemes. They provided no protection from any losses caused from the bad mortgages that companies like countrywide were developing. The result of selling trillions of dollars of these credit default swaps was to put into jeopardy the nature and existence of AIG, the world's largest insurance company. AIG was involved with almost every major corporation in the United States. Because of the risk, that these credit default swaps posed to AIG as well as to Goldman Sachs the entire economic system of the United

States was put into peril. This was the reason that AIG and others received hundreds of billions of dollars of bailout through the TARP program.

Except for the potential failure of the nine largest banks in the fall of 2008, the failure of AIG and Goldman Sachs would have been the next most serious financial issue facing our country. The corruption and misuse of power and the entanglement of government to allow this misuse to occur is one of the most damning of the broken promises of conservatives today.

Up until the economic collapse in the fall of 1929, it appeared as if the policies we were following which allowed large corporations and the very wealthy to operate in an unbridled fashion and without responsibility was producing prosperity for our country. We also instituted protectionist trade policies and tariffs that helped set the stage for the most fundamental economic catastrophe this country has ever experienced—The Great Depression. The dimensions of the economic morass created by the Great Depression are hard to imagine since very few people today lived through it. We had a country literally brought to its knees and had somewhere in the range of 25 to 30% unemployment as compared with the April 2014 rate of 6.3% and if you added underemployment in 1929 you would have reached more than 50% at the depths of the Great Depression.

We had people living on the streets standing in line waiting for a piece of bread and a small bowl of watered down soup. People who formally had worked hard and had a reasonable net worth were wiped out in a matter of several days. We had shantytowns constructed in major cities of our country because people had nowhere to live. All of this occurred because we allowed the unbridled misuse of money and power by wealthy individuals and large corporations in the years leading up to the fall of 1929. As bad, as the market crash was on 27 October 1929 the bank failure in many cases was even worse. It affected people that were of even more modest means who had their life savings in the banks that one day closed never to reopen.

My family had personal experience with this phenomenon when the Dime Savings Bank in Allentown Pennsylvania closed never to reopen. My great-grandmother on my maternal side lost, for the most part, all of her liquid assets when the Dime Savings Bank failed in 1933.There were millions of Americans who lost all or most of what they had when the banks failed.

http://en.wikipedia.org/wiki/File:American union bank.gif

We had no FDIC and no effective Federal Reserve. We had a system that for the most part allowed banks to take risks and operate without regulation, without control, and that excess along with the unregulated speculation in the stock market all but destroyed the economy of the most powerful nation on earth and brought with it a worldwide depression. Many conservatives today change the subject or refuse to knowledge that speculation and lack of effective regulation are the principal reasons why the Great Depression happened in the United States. They ignore the hands-off administrations of Coolidge and Hoover that enabled the Great Depression to take place. Conservatives also forget the impact of the Protectionist Tariffs on agricultural and industrial goods (Smoot-Hawley Tariff Act) which is another major cause of the Great Depression of 1929.

In January 1933, Franklin Delano Roosevelt was faced with a situation that, left unchecked, could have produced a system that would be more accurately described as a plutocracy. This group of the very wealthy and powerful people got the right politicians in office and judges on the courts to protect their wealth and power. Only the widespread economic consequences, which became known in the fall of 1929 and came to a head with the bank failure in early 1933, caused the people in this country to vote for progressive candidates and recognize the illusion that was created by Coolidge and Hoover and their conservative agenda that resulted in the Great Depression.

The concept of "the best government is the least government" which is one of the principal tenets of a conservatism was actually shown to be ineffective long before the 1900's and the robber barons. During the first 15 years of the United States, the government structure that we adopted under the Articles of Confederation where the central government had, almost no power or authority proved to be unworkable. It was because of that that realization that the Constitution replaced the ineffective Articles of Confederation in 1789.

Even though the Constitution passed in 1789 significantly strengthened the Federal Government through federalism much of the power was still in the hands of the individual states. Over the years, it became clear that as the United States changed from an agrarian society to a manufacturing and commercial society we needed to have more uniform procedures in order to grow and prosper. We could not afford 50 different sets of rules dealing with the growing economy and world commerce. Our Pledge of Allegiance clearly states, "One **nation** under God, indivisible with liberty and justice for all." We are not **50 nations** and the Liberty and Justice for All should be the same no matter which state we choose to live in and raise our families.

The Constitution provides to the states the authority not specifically enumerated in the Constitution to the Federal Government. The growth in power that was needed for the country to prosper, grow, and effectively deal on the world stage was achieved under the Commerce Clause in the Constitution. Whenever something related to the commerce of the country at large the Federal Government trumps state law and regulation.

If it were not for that interpretation, it is hard to imagine how the United States would function as ONE NATION! Those that claim we should get back to the founding fathers' employ rhetoric that although it sounds good it is in effect meaningless. Our country today is nothing like the country in 1776 or 1789 and if the founding fathers had been faced with the reality of the 21st century, I doubt very much that the Federalism that we have in our Constitution would exist to the extent that it does today.

So from the very founding of our country, the concept that we can allow individuals, companies and states to go it alone and do as they please has been proven to be not only ineffective but on a number of occasions disastrous. It is hard to know if Teddy Roosevelt had not confronted the robber barons what would have happened at the turn of the century. We saw the result that the lack of control and the concept that "business knows best," under Coolidge and Hoover, gave us in the fall of 1929. The near Depression in the fall of 2008 is the most recent example of the same lack of regulation. Failure to regulate Banks, AIG, Mortgage Originators and Mortgage Resellers, and Credit Default Swaps.

In 2020, by far the most immediate danger to our Republic comes from the actions of Donald J. Trump and the refusal of the Republicans in Congress to exercise their constitutional responsibility to uphold the Separation of Powers to deal with the actions of President Trump.

The unconstitutional actions of Mr. Trump that are endangering our country include:

1. **Seeking help from Russia to win the 2016 and 2020 elections.**
2. **Obstruction of Justice.**
3. **Lying**
4. **Demanding personal loyalty from agencies such as the DOJ and FBI.**
5. **Failure to follow the Constitution and abuse of power.**
6. **Encourage his followers to attack the Capitol and Congress to prevent it from completing the certification of the 2020 election.**

HOOVER CARTOONS
Description: Cartoon by Clifford K. Berryman,
published in the Washington Evening Star, 1917
Herbert Hoover Presidential Library and Museum
http://www.hoover.archives.gov/info/Food%20Relief/1917-58.html

That's all right, Mr. President.
We can just shake hands with ourselves.

http://www.ushistory.org/us/36b.asp

None of us today truly understand how serious the financial crisis our country was in between the fall of 1929 and early 1933. Many of the statistics that we have today did not exist in 1929 and it is difficult to really know the true extent of the unemployment and the underemployment that resulted by allowing unbridled speculation and irresponsible profiteering that took place prior to the fall of 1929.

It took the very aggressive centralization of government authority to begin taking our country back to a position of reason. The fact of the matter is we did not fully come out of the Great Depression until the Second World War. Actions like the CCC, WPA, rationing, price controls all were necessary to overturn the consequences that the laissez- faire policies of the Republicans under Coolidge and Hoover produced. The irony is that when the Great Depression took place many of the very wealthy lost much of their power and wealth. The unfortunate thing is that people who never had the power and the wealth also found they had almost nothing. This country had soup lines and shantytowns, which were dubbed Hooverville's. People who lived in these Hooverville's begged for food. There structures were made from wood from crates and cardboard or anything else that was available.

HOOVERVILLE
http://en.wikipedia.org/wiki/File:Hoooverville williamette.jpg

Despite the horrifying consequences of the Great Depression in 1929, we allowed ourselves to again jeopardize the economic system of our country with the policies we began to follow in 2001. We developed a similar scenario to the pre-1929 agenda when it appeared the economy was reasonably sound in the early part of the Bush administration up to late 2006 when the storm clouds became evident. The deficit began to grow with his tax cuts but the impact of the mortgage and investment bank abuses did not become evident until 2007. By September 2008, this country was on the brink of another Great Depression. We were within days of having our banks fail and the shutdown of the economic system of our country. In the days that led up to TARP, which was developed by Sec. of the Treasury Paulson, banks were in a position where they would not lend money to any person for any reason.

In the meetings that were held with George W. Bush and congressional leaders, Bush was told that if action was not taken to prop up the nine largest banks as well as AIG there was almost 100% probability of financial catastrophe similar to 1933. In fact, it is reported that at one of those meetings Sec. Paulson said to Bush that if he failed to act and convince Congress to pass TARP that he could very well have the legacy similar to Herbert Hoover except that the shantytowns that would result would be called Bushville's.

http://en.wikipedia.org/wiki/File:President George W. Bush bipartisan economic meeting Congress, McCain, Obama.jpg

Here again we saw the conservative ideology come into direct conflict with dealing effectively to prevent another Great Depression. When push came to shove, only six Republicans voted with the Democrats pass the TARP program and prevent a bank failure and the failure of AIG. The conservatives argued that the free market should deal with the problem, which was tantamount to saying that they should allow the banks and AIG to fail. The consequences that would follow, would be better than dealing with the crisis. It is hard to understand how any philosophical belief could be as fundamentally wrong as to risk repeating a situation similar to 1933.

It is important that we all understand just how serious of an economic morass was created by allowing big business and wealthy individuals to operate without reasonable and effective controls. Only in that way can we hope to prevent such a re-occurrence again. If today, the United States fell into an economic situation similar to the Great Depression the global impact would be nothing less than catastrophic for the entire planet.

Despite our history, in 2016 we elected a President and Congress who are ignoring the History of 1929 and 2008 and are repeating the same policies responsible for both these major economic disasters. Eliminating necessary regulation, cutting taxes for the wealthy and Big Business and Protective Tariff policies.

CHAPTER 2

THE NATURE OF CONSERVATISM

Although many of the tenets that comprise the conservative agenda in 2014 have existed in the past, the coalition of groups and individuals pushing these ideas has increased in intensity and ineffectiveness. Huge amounts of money from a few wealthy conservatives and a tactic of doing and saying almost anything in order to foster the conservative ideology has produced some very disturbing consequences.

Conservatism can be grouped into three specific areas. First, are the social conservatives which coalesce around things such as birth control, abortion and gay marriage and issues that relate to religious conviction rather than economic or foreign policy. Another group of conservative ideas centers around the role of the United States plays on the world stage with regard to foreign policy and military intervention. For the most part the Neocons, as they are known, are pushing a military solution to resolve many of the difficulties that exist throughout the world. The final and probably the most fundamental issues revolve around the role of government, which in turn dictates spending, and taxes.

In general, the issues that are dubbed of a social nature and that are based on religious belief are less subject to some of the broken promises that we see in the other two categories, foreign policy and the economy. Conservatives however are trying to enforce their ideology on everyone.

It is not satisfactory to simply hold these beliefs and practice them as they choose but rather to impose their beliefs on everyone else. A good example is the attempt to try to limit help to Planned Parenthood because of the belief that Planned Parenthood helps women with birth control and abortion should the women choose that option.

Certainly, the convection surrounding abortion and when life begins is a very fundamental issue and one that is difficult to deal with in the 21st century. Medical science and technology have enabled us to do things that heretofore were not possible or practical. Therefore, it is easier for women to opt for abortion to deal with an unwanted pregnancy or to utilize various methods of birth control to prevent the pregnancy in the first place. There is no argument that conservatives, as well as any other group, is certainly entitled to their individual belief and practice with respect to their sexuality, birth control and whom they choose to love. The issue is that the conservative movement attempts to impose their particular belief on everyone.

Free Will is granted to each person by God and should not be decided by anyone even when it deals with birth control or abortion. Some in the conservative movement believe that the sexuality of a person is a learned trait. This is simply incorrect, and science has established the fact that homosexuality is a reality both in human species as well as in other species.

The idea held by Michelle Bachmann and her husband who fostered a clinic to reeducate gays so that they would become heterosexual (normal to conservatives) is a perfect example of the conservative movement trying to impose what they believe on others. They do so despite the fact that the science simply does not support their particular belief and despite the reality, that God gave each of us are own free will. This is true of the global warming issue were 98% of the world scientists believe that the earth is warming and the vast majority of that 98% also believe that the actions of man burning hydrocarbons and increasing the CO_2 levels is accelerating the climate change. Despite the fact that 98% of the world's scientists are in agreement. We have indisputable facts that show that the temperatures of the oceans have risen, that the polar caps are melting, and the level of the world's oceans have risen. Conservative groups insist this is untrue and belittle science and the empirical data that proves climate change is taking place on planet Earth. The most likely reason conservatives are ignoring this reality is that to curb the amount of hydrocarbons pumped into the atmosphere will require more regulation, higher taxes and increasing costs for many businesses would be needed to implement solutions that will reduce carbon emissions.

The downside of ignoring the global warming issue could be nothing less than catastrophic. Two very important components must be addressed to avoid this catastrophe. We need defensive measures in low-lying areas to protect those areas from storm surges because the oceans are rising. Areas like New York, New England, the Gulf Coast and Florida are becoming increasingly vulnerable to the damage caused by the disruption of the Earth's weather patterns and the fact that the oceans have risen and will continue to rise. Unless we act like Holland and England within 50 to 100 years, we will not be able to use many of our coastal areas. The financial hardship this will cause the United States is unimaginable.

The second issue is how can we slow the onslaught of this climate change to not only give us the time to provide for some defensive measures but also to reduce the magnitude of the defensive measures that may be necessary. We need to protect the two thirds of the population that live along coastal areas. The downside of ignoring global warming will be the most fundamental mistake this country has made in its entire history. To envision the United States without New England, New York, the Gulf Coast, Florida and parts of California is unfathomable. We simply cannot risk allowing the conservative tactics to ignore the consequences of this issue. The consequences are such that we will be unable to continue as a world power and to enable our country to maintain its freedom if we had the catastrophic financial impact of losing our coastal areas because of rising oceans and the damage caused by ever intensifying storms.

We have other groups of conservatives who also argue that the earth and man is about 6,000 years old despite the fact that there is indisputable scientific evidence that life existed on the earth for hundreds and hundreds of millions of years. These conservative groups argue that there is no such thing as evolution and that about 6,000 years ago everything that we see from the simplest plant to the most complex organisms began. We see attempts by the conservatives to impose their ideas on others. The effort in Texas to change the textbooks to remove evolution is another good example of why conservatives insist that what they believe should be believed and accepted by everyone despite the fact that their beliefs are simply unsupportable by scientific data and facts. Certainly, there are no more compelling examples of how conservatives generally either ignore factual data that disproves their ideas or distorts actual data to make it appear as if their positions on various issues are valid. One of the tactics that is used is to repeat unsupportable statements and lies over and over again so that eventually people will begin to believe that there may be some truth in the statements that are being made.

There is no question that this tactic has worked and convinced many otherwise logically thinking individuals that what the conservatives claim is the truth regardless of the evidence in factual data to the contrary. Another tactic that is used is to attempt to change or alter history or to make it appear as if something that has been documented simply did not happen. Several examples that fall into this category are things like ignoring the impact that speculation and unbridled and irresponsible actions by wealthy individuals and large corporations had on enabling the Great Depression in 1929.

Today we have people blaming the fact that the federal government encouraged home ownership and that this caused the millions of failed mortgages that began to take place beginning in early 2007.

The fact of the matter is that home ownership for people who are qualified and financially able to own a home is the most powerful stimulus for our economic welfare and growth. What caused the unbelievable debacle in the real estate and mortgage industries are the unsound mortgages that were created from 2002 to 2006. Approximately 90% of the bad mortgages were created during that time. People that should not have been given mortgages because of their financial inability to pay the mortgages were made. The so-called designer mortgages and" no doc" loans enabled buyers to gain approval for mortgages that were far in excess of what they can actually be expected to pay in the long run. This was done by unscrupulous mortgage companies to add to their profits by increasing the size of the mortgage granted to individuals. Some of these mortgages started with a $1,000 a month payment and then jumped to $2,000 a month after three years and then to $3,000 per month after five years. What the mortgage originators did was qualify the person only for the $1,000 payment ignoring the likelihood that they would not be able to increase their mortgage payment over a five- year period by 300%.

The 'no-doc loans' were granted without verifying income, employment or any other basic information prior to granting the mortgage. All the buyer had to do is put a down payment of 20% or more of the purchase price. When real estate prices began to fall many of these "no doc" loans wound up underwater because the 20% equity that they established all but disappeared when the value of their real estate dropped by 40 or 50%.

If every one of the mortgages that have been created in the 2002-2006 had been given to people that were qualified buyers, we would not have seen the huge default of millions of mortgages that took place starting in early 2007 and triggered the largest economic downturns since the Great Depression.

The issue was not as conservatives claim that the government encouraged people to buy homes that caused the default on the mortgages. The issue is that mortgage originators, rating companies and mortgage re-purchasers such as Fannie and Freddie Mac allowed millions of unsound mortgages to be created. The lack of effective regulation and oversight allowed the creation of these unsound mortgages.

CHAPTER 3

BROKEN PROMISES—SUPPLY SIDE ECONOMICS AND BIG GOVERNMENT IS BAD

B eginning with the 1980 presidential campaign, we heard a great deal about the change that conservatives were trying to initiate with respect to the size of government, taxes, welfare reform and a whole host of the issues that conservatives embraced. Very often when we apply a title or name to something as multifaceted as political ideology we can misstate or misapply the term to certain groups or individuals.

This is certainly true with the term conservative or for that matter liberal.

The conservative ideology can be grouped into three basic categories. The first category of issues that conservatives support is like the doorway to their Temple. One pillar is the idea that we have very limited government and that the free market is best suited to make the decisions without government interference.

This idea of supply-side economics where we tax the wealthy at a very low rate with the promise of trickle-down economic benefit to the remainder of our citizens. The second category is the social issues, which include birth control, abortion, women's healthcare, help for the poor, disabled, students and gay-rights. Finally, the third area relates to the foreign policy issues and the use of our military to impose solutions in the world's trouble spots. Today Terrorism is the major danger we face while Communism was the issue during the 1960-1980's. There are some people who would consider themselves conservatives who support the conservative position in all of these categories while others concentrate on only some of these policies.

For example, the most extreme group regarding the role of government is the Libertarians, which for the most part would have very little government of any sort. Many of the people in this particular category do not have a strong feeling about some of the social issues. Nevertheless, all of these policy areas are in stark contrast to what most progressives embrace and the reasons we are having such political discord. There is very little middle ground given the extreme differences between what the conservatives would have us do and what the progressives want. American politics in 2020 is like having a switch that has two positions on or off. There is no dimmer switch especially with respect to what the conservatives are willing to accept.

One of the most fundamental issues comes from the first category and deals with the concept known as supply side economics. During the 1980 campaign, Ronald Reagan made a very effective argument that in essence says by lowering the tax rates for the upper income Americans we would stimulate economic growth and provide a stronger economy. The idea was that the wealthy would utilize their additional resources from lower taxes to invest in businesses, create jobs and the benefits would trickle down from the top to the middle class and provide a broadening of the economic benefits.

This concept was dubbed "Reaganomics" and it was a very significant departure from what we had been doing and from the theory that most economic growth and prosperity is a factor of demand and spending. Certainly, we did not have a lack of capital for business investment prior to 1981 when we had significantly higher tax rates on the upper income taxpayer. American Business never lacked the capital it needed to grow and expand.

Ronald Reagan was a very effective speaker and his ability to sell his supply-side economics and the smaller government concept probably stems from his years as an actor in Hollywood. During the debates of the 1980 presidential election, he was very effective in convincing both the American voter and later the democratically controlled Congress to put in place his ideas. This came at a time when we had relatively high taxes, which had been even higher in the 40s, 50s and 60s because of the horrendous cost that the Second World War placed on the United States.

http://en.wikipedia.org/wiki/File:Carter Reagan Debate 10-28-80.png

President Reagan convinced Congress to enact his plan to reduce the top tax rate from 70% to 28% and end the indexing for inflation that had been part of the tax law. The impact on the revenue from these changes was huge and President Reagan understood that initially there would be an annual budget deficit because of the loss in tax revenue.

The two promises made by conservatives were if we cut the tax rates as President Reagan wanted, by 1985, growth in economy would restore the lost revenue due to the tax cuts and the budget would be balanced.

The second promise was that the benefits would trickle down to the middle class with job and GDP growth and produce economic benefits for all Americans due to the tax cuts for the wealthy.

As expected, the annual budget deficit began to grow and continued to grow through the entire term of President Reagan's eight years in office. Below per the Bureau of Public Debt, Department of the Treasury are the actual results from the implementation of Reaganomics:

Table 1.4

Year	Annual Budget Deficit* (Amounts in Billions)
1981	86
1982	134
1983	231
1984	218
1985	266
1986	283
1987	222
1988	253
Total	1,693 ($1.7 Trillion)

*Does not include revenue or expense from Social Security or Medicare. Source OMB Historical

The total impact on the National Debt during the eight years of Ronald Reagan presidency after passing his huge tax cuts, took the debt from approximately $907Billion to $2.6 Trillion. That is an increase of almost 300% in eight years.

Clearly the promise that by 1985 the budget would return to be in balance after the Reagan tax cuts was not kept. The reason that the promise failed is because the growth and the trickle-down to the middle class in the form of better paying jobs and more benefits to

Middle-class Americans failed to materialize in anything close to what Ronald Reagan had promised when selling his supply-side economics to the American voter and to Congress. Thus, both the promise of a balance budget and the trickle-down benefits to the middle and lower income Americans simply never happened. What did happen is the wealthy became wealthier and the indebtedness of the country tripled. (Source:www.treasurydirect.gov/govt/reports/pd/histdebt/ histdebt.htm)

If the impact of failing to keep these two conservative promises from the Reagan tax cuts had ended when Ronald Reagan left office, their impact would not have been so devastating on the United States. The truth of the matter is that Ronald Reagan was very disappointed by the budget deficits and agreed to raise taxes several times in the latter part of his administration in order to reduce the ever-growing deficit that resulted from his 1981 tax cuts.

The irony is that any Republican candidate in 2020 that acted like Ronald Reagan who admitted his mistake and increases taxes to help move the budget back toward balance would be crucified by the conservatives. Can you imagine any of the leading conservative Republican candidates in 2014 or the 2016 that would support increasing taxes in order to help balance the budget? Any such assertion by Donald Trump in 2020 would be the kiss of death. Although most Republicans have canonized Ronald Reagan, anyone acting like Ronald Reagan in the latter part of his presidency could not be elected Republican dogcatcher today.

When George H. W. Bush was elected president and took office, he made his famous promise, "read my lips no new taxes." President Bush quickly learned that even with the increase in taxes that Ronald Reagan approved it was not possible to bring the budget to balance given the tax rates that were in place when he took office. Bush 41 was probably the last major Republican leader who was truly a fiscal conservative. When he saw it was not possible to move toward a balanced budget given the low tax rates, he went back on his promise and raised taxes in order to help move the country toward a balanced budget. For him, balancing the budget was the prime directive as it would be for any truly fiscal conservative person. The so-called fiscal conservatives today are nothing of the sort. They are simply anti-tax.

In addition to the added revenue from the Bush tax increases, we saw President Bush reduce spending especially on the military taking advantage of the peace dividend after the collapse of the Soviet Union. The rate of increase in the national debt began to slow and by the end of Bush 41's term in office the national debt stood at approximately $4.1 Trillion. Thus in his four years the national debt rose approximately $1.1 Trillion. Nevertheless, when George Herbert Walker Bush left office the United States was still running an annual budget deficit of about $380 billion per year. (Source:www.treasurydirect. gov/govt/ reports/pd/histdebt/histdebt.htm)

When President Bill Clinton took office, he also found that even with the increases in taxes from Ronald Reagan and Bush 41, we were still running substantial deficits. Even the spending cuts were not sufficient to return the budget to balance. As a result, Bill Clinton, like his two predecessors, increased taxes and further cut spending especially on the military in order to bring the budget into balance. The annual budget deficit continued to drop and by 2000, we had the first balanced budget in decades. It took 18 years to end the annual deficits the Reagan tax cuts created. The cumulative impact of the Reagan tax cuts on the national debt was to take our national debt from $900 billion in 1980 to $5.7 trillion in 2000. Thus, the real impact on the national debt from the disastrous Reaganomics was almost $5 trillion increase in the national debt.

The long-term consequences of increasing the national debt by $5 trillion, assuming that the interest we would have to pay is about 5% would be $250 billion a year in added interest. Although today we have very low interest rates according to the Department of the Treasury Bureau Public Debt, the average that we have paid on our public debt over the years averages about 5%. There is no reason to believe that in the long run we will not see the cost to finance our national debt return to that 5% rate. Therefore, the actual impact of just the Reagan experiment with supply-side economics has had a huge impact on our budget and will continue to do so until we have repaid that debt. If interest rates were to go above 5%, as they were during the early Reagan years, the negative impact on our budget will be even greater.

In 2001, George W. Bush became our first president with an MBA from Harvard, nonetheless. In 2001, President Bush argued that we had a projected surplus in the neighborhood of $6 trillion that would materialize between 2001 and 2011. He therefore reasoned that we were overtaxing the American taxpayer because of this $6 trillion projected surplus and proposed his 2001 tax cuts to Congress. The Bush tax cuts were to stimulate the economy, create jobs and trickle down to the masses. It was precisely the same promises that Ronald Reagan made 20 years earlier.

The 2001 Bush tax cut was designed to benefit the top 10% of taxpayers. We were given a warning from none other than Alan Greenspan, chairman of the Federal Reserve that we should never again return to annual budget deficits now that we had finally balanced the budget. In fact, Alan Greenspan, a lifelong Republican, said that if the proposed tax cuts were passed and we again returned to annual budget deficits that the tax cuts should be rescinded. (Source www. reprints.longform.org/alan-greenspan-hylton1/25/2001) At the same time, the two wealthiest men on earth, Bill Gates and Warren Buffett, sent a letter to President George W. Bush recommending he not cut the tax revenue by lowering income tax rates. They said we had far more important things to do with the money. Bush insisted that we were overtaxing the American public and justified giving most of the tax cuts to the wealthy since the wealthy were the ones that pay most of the income taxes.

President Bush and the Republicans controlled House and Senate passed the 2001 tax cut, which lowered taxes primarily on the wealthiest Americans. The result of the 2001 Bush tax cuts was to immediately cause the annual budget deficit to return. We went from a small surplus in 2000 to a $100 billion deficit in 2001. In 2002, that deficit jumped to $360 billion. Even with a strong economy, the Bush tax cuts caused a return to annual budget deficits. Rather than follow the advice of Alan Greenspan and rescind the 2001 tax cut, George Bush and the Republican-controlled Congress passed a second tax cut in 2003 and the deficit began growing even faster. Then GWB invaded Afghanistan and Iraq, which increased military spending and drove the annual budget even higher.

By the end of the eight years of the Bush presidency, the annual budget deficit stood at over $1.5 trillion. George W. Bush pushed the national debt from the roughly $5.7 trillion when he took office to $11.9 trillion. That is an increase of more than $6 trillion, which is the exact amount that Bush claimed in his projected surplus. The truth of the matter is there was no surplus and again we applied of the same conservative supply-side economics that produced the same result. What a surprise!

Thus, the conservatives tried their supply-side economics three times by cutting taxes in 1981, 2001 and 2003. Each time the conservative promise of a balanced budget and trickle-down benefits failed. Each time we got the very same result even though the promise of the conservatives was to give us the opposite result. When you look at the magnitude of the increase in the National Debt that doing the same thing repeatedly did to our indebtedness the lunacy of the conservative agenda with respect to our budget and our national debt is irrefutable. This is not opinion. This is not theory. It is what happened when we cut revenue to the point where we could no longer pay for the spending that the Congress and the President agreed to spend each and every year. This increase in the National Debt had absolutely nothing to do with either Social Security or Medicare. In fact, during the period from Ronald Reagan through Bush 43, both Social Security and Medicare generated annual surpluses. Although these entitlement programs are definitely, a long-term funding issue they played absolutely no part in taking our national debt from less than $1 trillion in 1980 to just under $12 trillion in 2008.

Most of the increase in our debt is because of the failed conservatives Supply-Side Economics. Add to that the increased spending on two wars conservatives refused to fund with added tax revenue.

In 2009, Barack Obama was handed the largest budget deficit in our history. In addition, the economy was on the brink of another 1929. He was also confronted with a challenge from the Republicans to the Wisconsin senatorial seat of Al Franken. This prevented Democrats from controlling the 60 votes in the Senate to stop Republican Filibusters.

For the first five months of President Obama's term in office, nothing of substance passed in the United States Senate because the Republicans employed the filibuster to prevent a vote. There is no question the policy changes would have been approved by the Senate if it had come to a vote but this parliamentary maneuver known as filibusters that requires 60 votes to bring a bill to a vote continued the policies of George W. Bush.

In addition to the inability to increase taxes or pass a Stimulus package in January 2009, President Obama was faced with the added cost of the two Bush wars, which were raging at a cost of hundreds of billions of dollars per year. The near depression President Obama inherited from George W. Bush meant that millions of Americans who lost their jobs were no longer paying income taxes and began drawing welfare benefits because of the unprecedented economic disaster that George W. Bush handed his successor.

In May 2009, the disputed Wisconsin seat was settled and Al Franken was seated as the 60th Democratic Senator. At that point, President Obama began by passing his economic stimulus measures to reverse the economic downturn he had inherited. The Democratically controlled House and Senate passed a stimulus package, which was approximately $800 billion. It was equally split between tax cuts to the middle class, direct payments to the states and infrastructure repair projects.

By the time, the stimulus package began to show some impact we were at the beginning of the second year of President Obama's first term in office. Conservatives claimed that the stimulus package would not work and was not needed. The fact remains, by the second year of President Obama's term we saw an end to the loss in jobs and a reduction in the annual budget deficit from the $1.5 trillion level that he inherited in 2009 to $ 650 Billion in 2014. The Stimulus did work even though most economists believe, given the magnitude of the recession Bush handed Obama, the stimulus was too small.

In November 2009, the special election to replace the late Ted Kennedy's seat in the Senate produced a shock to President Obama when a Republican, Scott Brown, was elected to fill the balance of Ted Kennedy's term. At that point, the remainder of any changes to help stimulate the economy or reform our tax laws came to an end because Republicans again return to their tactic of filibustering almost everything President Obama proposed. The consequence was President Obama became almost like a Lame Duck one year into his first term. The national debt continued to grow at a slower pace. By 2014 the national debt stood at $17 ½ trillion dollars. The inability to further stimulate the economy and increase tax revenue by restoring tax rates to a more reasonable level and ending tax loopholes has extended the tax policies enacted by Bush and the conservatives. This has prevented us from balancing the budget and continued increasing the National Debt from $12 Trillion in 2009 to over $31 Trillion today.

The bottom line of the conservative promise that supply-side economics and cutting taxes on the wealthiest taxpayers would balance the budget and grow the economy to the benefit of the middle class has been an abject failure. All the data clearly shows that the promises made simply were not kept. During the eight years of Bill Clinton's administration, we created approximately 22,000,000 private-sector jobs. During the eight years that followed under George W. Bush we created a net of 1 million new private-sector jobs. When George Bush left office, we were losing in excess of 700,000 jobs per month. As soon as he impacts of the Obama stimulus package began to take effect we reversed the job loss and took it from a 700,000 loss per month to an average gain of about 200,000 jobs per month. We added

8.9 million Private sector jobs through April 2014. (Source. Bureau of Labor Statistics).

Today given the fact that conservatives continue to hold on to the discredited supply-side economics that has failed this country on three separate occasions in the last 39 years. We continue to run annual budget deficit over a Trillion dollars per year prior to the corona virus. Thus, every two years will add another $2 trillion to the national debt simply because of the refusal of the conservative members of Congress to recognize the impact of their policies and admit that we need to return to a tax burden that will enable us to pay our bills. The last two budgets passed by the Republican House are a continuation of the supply-side economics that failed our country over and over again. Both of the Ryan budgets that passed the House would cut spending at a time when we are trying to stimulate the economy and give even greater tax cuts to the wealthiest Americans. Thus, the conservatives have learned absolutely nothing from the experiences of 1981, 2001, 2003 and 2017. They make believe the near depression that came to a head in September 2008 and in 2020 is somehow a "miraculous conception" for which they have no responsibility. Truly the policy of the conservatives to again and again to cut taxes for the wealthy in this country with the promise that it will benefit the country and balance the budget is insanity.

Another of the conservative promises is that less regulation will result in higher growth and economic benefits to all Americans. Conservatives promised this would stimulate the growth of small business and help the middle class obtain living wage jobs. Conservatives argue the way to prosperity is to let the free market operate with little or no federal regulation so that they can unleash the entrepreneurial spirit that will produce a better life for all.

Let us take a look at what has taken place when we have allowed the wealthy and powerful to operate with little or no regulation or control. During the Golden age at the turn-of-the-century, we saw the robber barons operate in a ruthless manner to the detriment of millions and millions of the average Americans. We saw country moving toward an oligarchy in which a handful of people were able to control the elected officials and pass laws that benefited themselves at the expense of others. During the 1920s, we had the same concept under Coolidge and Hoover that allowed the free market to operate virtually unfettered and with little regulation. We saw banks act in ways that were irresponsible.

We allowed speculation on the securities market that produced a level of greed that was a kin to gambling.

In the fall of 1929, this uncontrolled and unbridled greed in the securities markets produce the largest single economic catastrophe ever to befall the United States of America. The Great Depression saw the collapse first of the securities markets in the fall of 1929 and in 1933 the failure of many banks. Between these two occurrences both wealthy and not so wealthy lost most or all of their accumulated assets and wealth. Millions became dependent on the government and were reduced to utter poverty and despair.

Only through very aggressive policies were we able to slowly crawl out of the hole that was created by the Great Depression. In fact, we were still in a serious recession at the onset of World War II. We finally ended the Great Depression and its devastating impact on our society due to the fact that our country became embroiled in the largest world war in the history of humankind.

Clearly the conservative promise that allowing the free market to operate with little control or regulation resulted in the disaster known as Great Depression. Following the Depression, Progressives were successful in regaining control of the government and passing laws and regulations to protect individuals and our economic system. Laws were passed to regulate the securities industries as well as the banks. These laws recognized that we could not allow the banks, stock market and big business to operate as the conservatives supported with little regulation or control.

Following the Second World War this country grew at a substantial rate and became the most powerful economic country the earth has ever seen. We had periods of economic slowdowns, which we term business cycles and we had periods when inflation and economic stagnation did impact our country. However, nothing close to the Great Depression was experienced after the Second World War. During the Eisenhower administration, we began investing in the infrastructure with the interstate highway system. This was in addition to the infrastructure we built as part of the recovery from the Great Depression. All of this investment created jobs and produced long-term infrastructure that was needed for our country to grow and for our population to enjoy their leisure activities.

During the 1960s, we embarked on the space program another investment, which produced significant innovations that enabled companies to make new products and prosper. This continued up until the early 1980s when we began to again develop large deficits and cut spending especially on the military, which had been part of the stimulus to keep the economy growing. During the period of the 70s and 80s, we added very little to our infrastructure. We in fact began using up the infrastructure that we had previously built.

During the 1990s, we enjoyed a period where there were no major military conflicts and we moved, for the first time in decades, toward a balanced budget. During the eight years, President Clinton was in office our country saw both the wealthy and the middle class prosper. Unemployment was relatively low and we created 22 million private- sector jobs between 1992 and 2000 per the Bureau of Labor Statistics. In 2001 with the election of George W. Bush as president and the Republican controlled Congress the policies of the United States changed drastically. Regulation was relaxed and taxes were cut. The deficit ballooned and the stock market went from 14,000 in 2001 to 7,000 in early 2009.

We created 9 million private sector jobs during the first six years of the Bush administration, which is less than half the rate as under

Clinton. Then we lost approximately 8 million of those 9 million jobs during the economic collapse that developed in the last two years Bush as in office. The net result was that during the eight years of George W. Bush we created a net of 1 million jobs compared with the 22 million jobs created in the preceding eight years under Clinton. The Job Growth in nearly 32 years of Democratic president since Truman took office shows an additional 57.7 million. Job growth in 36 years of Republican presidents added 34.6 million. George W. Bush had 8/10 of one percent job growth. Bill Clinton 20.7% and Obama to date is at 12% or 8.9 Million jobs during the past 5 years.

Another promise of the conservatives is that the economy, job growth and the stock market do better when we have Republican administrations with lower taxes and less regulation. Let us take a look at how past history looks during both Republican and Democratic administrations.

How the Dow Jones Industrial Average performed during various presidential administrations:

President	Party	Average change per year in DOW
Obama	D	+25.0%
Clinton	D	+16.5%
Reagan	R	+11.2%
Eisenhower	R	+10.2%
GHWB	R	+10.7%
Truman	D	+ 9.4%
FDR	D	+ 8.0%
Ford	R	+ .2%
Nixon	R	+ .1%
Carter	D	- 1.1%
GWB	R	- 2.0%
Hoover	R	- 29.0%

JOB and GDP Growth

Job Growth

Average Job Gains per Month (Thousands)

Clinton	241.96
Carter	219.4
Johnson	192.4
Reagan	165.76
Nixon	140.13
Kennedy	104.12
Obama	93.8
Ford	62.52
Bush II	53.94
Eisenhower	42.84
Bush II	21.35

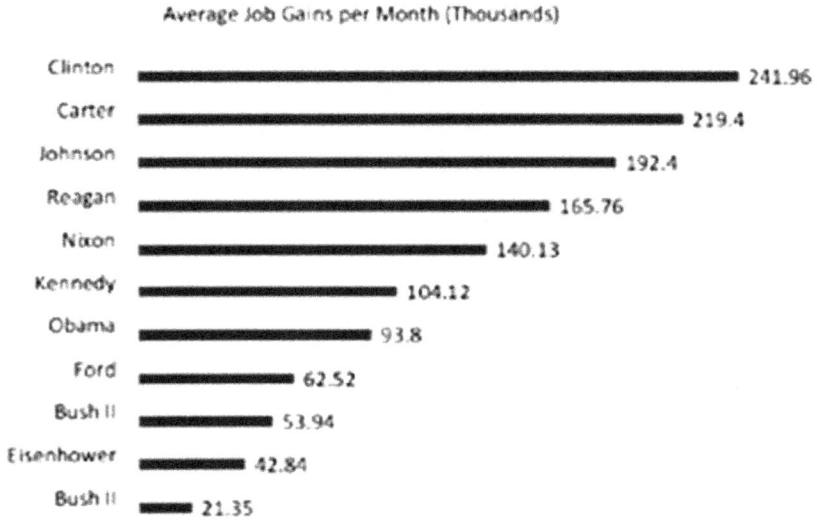

SOURCE: BUREAU OF LABOR STATISTICS

Economic Growth

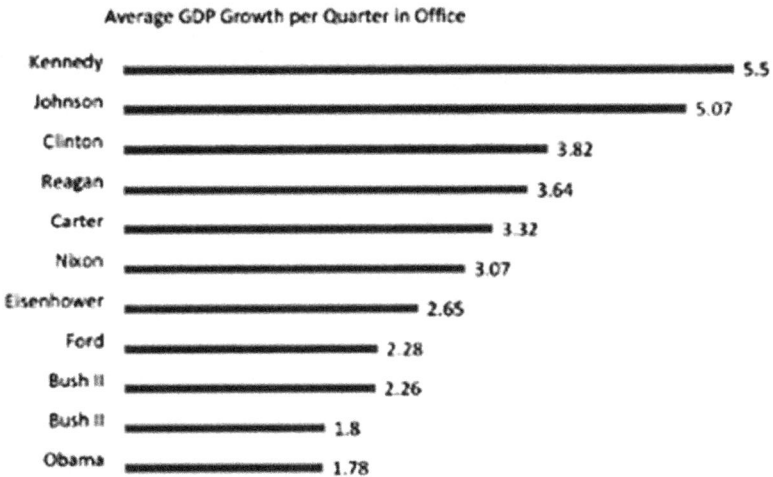

Average GDP Growth per Quarter in Office

Kennedy	5.5
Johnson	5.07
Clinton	3.82
Reagan	3.64
Carter	3.32
Nixon	3.07
Eisenhower	2.65
Ford	2.28
Bush II	2.26
Bush II	1.8
Obama	1.78

SOURCE: BUREAU OF ECONOMIC ANALYSIS

Job Growth so far under Trump is slightly lower than Obama and the GDP Growth rate is about the same as under Obama despite the claim by Trump that GDP growth around 2% was puny and growth under him would be between 4-5%.

Pete Souza; http://en.wikipedia.org/wiki/ File: Obama signs health care-20100323.jpg

The above data on the stock market performance, job creation and growth in the Gross Domestic Product (GDP) clearly show that the promise that business and the economy grow better under a Republican administration again is a promise not kept. In fact, our country has done significantly better from an economic and business perspective during Democratic administrations.

How many times will the conservatives repeat the claim that lower taxes on the wealthy create jobs and economic growth? No matter how many times they tell us that business does better during Republican administrations with less regulation and lower taxes we see from the above data this claim is untrue. Again, how many times will we have to accept the promises of a better tomorrow if only we adopt conservative policies?

Another very important example of the way the conservative promises have been unfulfilled is with the mortgage crisis that became evident beginning in 2007. This concept the conservatives hold is that we should allow business to operate with little or no oversight or regulation for they know best. This concept that the least government is the best government has brought our country to the economic abyss in 1929 and again 2008.

This idea allowed the mortgage crisis to develop and threaten the entire economy of this country and the world. What we saw in the past was mortgage creation by the banks that held them and assumed the risk when mortgage holders failed to make the required payments. When this was the case, there was some self-policing by the banks because they had their money at risk. Over the past 20 to 30 years, there has been a change in the way mortgages are created in the United States. Mortgage brokers create the mortgage for the express purpose of resale and do not hold a mortgage or take onto themselves any risk of default. In addition, the amount that the mortgage originators make is dependent on the size of the mortgage. A mortgage of $300,000 pays twice commission as a mortgage of $150,000. What we have is the Fox in the Hen House without any effective government regulation. These mortgage originators were free to operate in a way that resulted in the creation of millions of unsound mortgages just so they could make outrageous profits.

We have some conservatives trying to lay the blame on the government's encouragement for people to own homes. The Dodd/Frank laws are cited as having created the mortgage crisis when in fact nothing could be further from the truth. Homeownership is a driving force in our economy. There is nothing more important to the economic welfare and the growth of our country then homeownership by people who can actually afford the home. Dodd/ Frank did not encourage mortgages that were unsound; they encouraged homeownership by people who were able to pay for their home and mortgage. It was the greedy mortgage originators that created unsound mortgages simply to make a bigger profit with no effective government oversight or regulation, which was in keeping with the conservative agenda.

There were two types of mortgages that created our problems. One type of mortgage is called liar loans or "no doc" loans. Almost anyone was able to obtain a mortgage if they had 20% of the purchase price without any proof that they could afford to make the mortgage payments. As the price of homes began to fall 40-50%, the 20% down was no protection for the owner of the "no-doc" mortgages. The second type of problem mortgage that was developed by the mortgage origination industry was called designer mortgages. These were mortgages that in the initial few years had payments were artificially low and individuals were qualified only on the lowest payment for the first few years of the mortgage. In many cases within two or three years, the monthly mortgage payment doubled and in some cases at the end of five years, the payments increased another 50%. It was not unusual to have $1,000 payment go to $2,000 at the end of three years and then to $3,000 at the end of the fifth year of the mortgage.

The result of these loans was obvious. Millions of people were unable to afford the increased payments on these mortgages and they began to go into default. These unsound mortgages for the most part was created from 2002 through 2006. They were not the result of encouraging people to buy homes. It was the result of not regulating the mortgage origination companies and allowing them to operate simply to make the most profit that they can possibly make even though they were creating unsound mortgages in the process. These unsound mortgages were bundled with conventional mortgages and rated by companies like Standard & Poor's and Moody's who found that they could make billions in fees from the ratings. Many of the bundles of mortgages were rated as sound when in fact many of the mortgages within those bundles were unsound. Again, there was little or no regulation on how these mortgage bundles were rated.

These bundles were then resold in the secondary market principally through Fannie Mae and Freddie Mac and here again the conservative principles were clearly in play because there was little or no regulation on what types of mortgages these repurchases could buy. If they had been restricted to repurchase loans that were qualified on a conventional basis for the entire period of mortgage payments i.e. the $1,000, $ 2,000 or $3,000 payments, these unsound designer mortgages would not have been created. If the mortgage originators had been unable to sell the unsound mortgages they had created, they would have been forced to take on the risk from default. This would have prevented mortgage originators creating these unsound mortgages.

Finally, some enterprising insurance companies like AIG decided that they could make hundreds of billions of dollars by selling a thing called a Credit Default Swaps. These Ponzi schemes were not designed to protecting the banks but simply to make huge profits for the companies selling these worthless promises. Credit default swaps were sold to reimburse a bank holding a bad mortgage should they fail. They were written in such a way to avoid being construed as insurance and Congress was prevented from either regulating them through the SEC or even all having oversight into this entire market because of a conservative amendment tacked on to a 2000 Bill.

Here we have an example not only of failing to control or regulate this Ponzi scheme but the government actually was prevented from doing anything including oversight so companies like AIG could operate without interference. When mortgages began to fail by the hundreds of thousands and AIG was asked with reimburse the mortgage holders they were placed into a position of jeopardy that could have destroyed AIG. At that time, AIG insured all types of risks for most of the Fortune 500 corporations in the United States.

All of this is a perfect example of the failure of the conservative promise that we should allow business to act by itself and without government regulation. Not only did the conservative promise fail but also that failure jeopardized the entire economic structure of the United States. It took the bailout of the banks and AIG as well as very aggressive action by the Federal Reserve and FDIC to prevent this country from falling into another Great Depression simply because we allowed mortgage originators rating company's mortgagor's byers and insurance companies to act in ways that were irresponsible and refused to establish effective regulation and oversight.

We constantly hear from the conservatives the federal bureaucracy is ever expanding and that big government is bad for the American taxpayer and the economy. In part, this is an example not so much of a failed promise of a blatant untruth. The fact of the matter is that the employment and the size of government in absolute numbers is the lowest that is been in 47 years. We have to go back to 1966 to find a smaller federal government. **Today federal workers constitute 2% of the nation's total labor force in 1966 federal employees accounted for 4.3% of the American workforce. Despite the facts, the conservatives continue to complain about big government, which is simply a lie.**

Federal Government workers (in thousands) from the Office of Personnel Management:

1966	5,888
1980	4,965
1992	4,931
2000	4.129
2008	4,206
2014	2,046
2017	2,088

What the conservatives are saying is we can prove that government is bigger because it's spending more. This is all part of their philosophy to cut government spending whenever possible. The truth of the matter is that much of the federal budget is subject to inflation. Every one of the 2.7 million federal workers get a raise each year in addition to the 1.4 million Military. Federal retirees both civilian and military get a Cost of Living Allowance (COLA), which increases the spending at the federal government level. Everything the government buys goes up in price whether it is for food, clothing, and gasoline. When the government contracts for work the cost of inflation to contractors drives up the cost of the federal government. When in2007-2008 we had a loss of 8 million jobs and people began drawing unemployment and food stamps federal spending went up. That did not mean that the size of government increased. It simply means that the number of dollars our government had to spend to deal with the economic disaster increased. This conservative concept that big government is bad does dovetail into another broken conservative promise that it is good to cut the budget and that will help our economy. The truth of the matter is that the spending cuts since 2011 have cost 1 million government jobs per the CBO. That means that those million people and their families cut their spending that does harm to the economy. Many of the government workers that lost their jobs started drawing unemployment, which increased federal spending. This idea that government spending does not create jobs and does not stimulate the economy is simply a broken promise and a lie being told to us by the conservatives.

When the federal government spends a dollar, it generally goes to private contractors to buy things or provide services. That money turns into salary wages and profits. It is as if the conservatives want us to believe every time the government spends a dollar it goes into the black hole of Calcutta. When the government spends money, the multiplier effect produces economic growth jobs profits and economic well-being. **We should not pay for the added spending by increasing our debt and the interest to service that debt. The solution is to increase our tax revenue so as we can "pay as we go" for the things that we need and for the investments to help our country grow. We do that by**

asking those making huge sums of money to pay more and return to the pre-1981 tax rates and eliminate or minimize the loopholes, which enable the wealthy to avoid paying their fair share of taxes. When you have someone like Mitt Romney with a $20 Million dollar annual income paying only 14% we see a person who in not meeting his responsibility to our country.

Despite the fact, conservatives claim we need to create more jobs their budget policies are producing the exact opposite result and they are therefore not keeping the promise that spending cuts will help our economy.

While the conservatives complain that job growth has not been, rapid enough they have refused to approve the jobs bill President Obama proposed more than two years ago. According to the CBO, this jobs bill, which is primarily infrastructure repair, would've added 2 million living wage private sector jobs. Thus, the promise that spending cuts and their refusal to invest in our country is good for the country is incorrect.

The conservative refusal to provide added government spending for police, firefighters, teachers and infrastructure repair has cost at least 3 million jobs per the Congressional Budget Office (CBO). In addition, their refusal to extend the unemployment benefits according to the CBO will cost another 330,000 jobs.

The list goes on which clearly demonstrates over and over again the conservative dogma and policies that they repeat over and over again are not keeping the promise of a better life for the majority of Americans. To the contrary, we would be further down the pike to a balanced budget with 3 million more people working and corporations would have the added profits from all the infrastructure repairs. All this would increase the tax revenue and reduce the annual budget deficit.

Even if the infrastructure repairs were not needed to create jobs they are needed to keep in repair things that we use every day in both our commercial and personal lives. At the present time, there are approximately 63,000 bridges that desperately need repair. If Congress does not act, there will be no money to continue road repair in the United States. The conservatives' refusal to invest in our country and repair our infrastructure carried to extreme will bring us huge economic problems in the future. In addition to the 63,000 bridges that need repair, we have more than 4,000 dams in need of work. In May 2020, we saw four dams fail in Michigan. We have antiquated and ineffective power transmission systems. Many of our sewer and water systems in our major cities are in excess of 100 years old.

Rather than ask the wealthy to pay higher taxes and invest that money to rebuild our infrastructure, the conservatives insist that government spending is not necessary and would not create jobs. Even if the spending on our infrastructure did not create a single new job, the fact is our infrastructure needs to be repaired.

There is no part of the conservative agenda that is moving this country forward to create jobs, increase GDP growth or help the middle class in our country. The policies they support and have proposed for the future, as reflected in the last two budgets that passed the House of Representatives benefit only the wealthy while cutting the safety net for the people in need. The top 10% have done well over the last 10 to 12 years and the top 5% extremely well. The increase in wealth of the top 1% is off the scale. Despite the growth that we have seen for the very wealthy in our country, we still have conservative multibillionaire's complaining about the role of government and the Obama policies.

Some very pointed examples of wealthy conservatives and their distorted view of the federal government include Sheldon Adelson, CEO of Las Vegas Sands Corporation. Mr. Adelson reportedly had a net worth when President Obama took office of approximately $3 billion. Today he is reportedly worth somewhere in the neighborhood of $37 billion. Despite this fact, he complains bitterly about government regulation and the policies of Barack Obama. He is a man that wants the federal government to regulate online gambling to help protect his casino empire. His net worth reportedly has gone up approximately 13 times yet he complains about the way government prevents business from prospering and growing.

Another example is the Koch brothers who also bitterly complain about President Obama and his progressive policies. Their net worth reportedly went from $38 billion when President Obama took office to $77 billion today. These two brothers spent over $400 million in the last presidential election to defeat President Obama's reelection.

Yet a third conservative billionaire who constantly blasts President Obama and his policies is Kenneth Langdon, cofounder of Home Depot. Here is another example of a man whose net worth has reportedly doubled since President Obama took office.

All of these and other conservative billionaires have very short memories. These wealthy conservatives as well as all other Americans should think back to September 2008 and the near Depression that resulted after eight years of conservative control. The fall of 2008 was a kin to the fall of 1929. Only because of the action to approve TARP, the aggressive action of the Federal Reserve and the FDIC as well as the stimulus package did we avoid another Great Depression. Donald Trump in repeating the same conservative policies that risk the onset of yet a third major economic disaster similar to 1929 and 2008. Cutting necessary regulations on banks and financial institutions, environmental regulations and global warming, tax cuts that only benefit the wealthy and Big Business while driving up the National Debt and the imposition of Protectionist Tariffs that risk a Trade War. His refusal to support fully funding Social Security, deal with Health Care and rebuild the infrastructure round out the dangers the Trump Presidency economic policies are causing our country!

The final straw was Trump's refusal to deal with the corona19 virus that he was warned about in min-November 2019 by our Intelligence Agencies. Until the end of February 2020, he was calling the virus a Democratic Hoax and it would just go away. On February 26, 2020 Trump said, "Within a couple of weeks it will be down to zero. That's a pretty good job we've done." On February 28th

Trump called the Corona Virus a "Democratic Hoax." On March 29th Trump said, "If we have between 100,000 and 200,000 deaths, we've done a very good job."

This is why the virus had such a devastating impact:

In 2017, Trump ignored the Pandemic role-play. In 2017, Trump ignored the Pandemic Playbook.
In 2018, Trump fired the Pandemic Response Team. In 2018, Trump cut the budget for CDC.
In 2019, Trump ignored the Intelligence warnings about the virus. In 2020, Trump refused the WHO Test Kits.
On February 28, 2020, Trump called it a Democratic Hoax.

The man who claimed to be the world's best dealmaker:

No deal with North Korea. No deal with China.
No deal with Iran.
No deal on Infrastructure Repair. No deal on Immigration.
No deal on Healthcare.
The Trade deal with Canada and Mexico is 90% the same as the NAFTA agreement Trump blasted.

The Art of the Deal is a FRAUD!

As of April 2021, 566,000 Americans have died from the Corona Virus.

CHAPTER 4

BROKEN PROMISES—SOCIAL ISSUES

S ome of the most contentious policies of the conservatives revolve around social issues. The attempts to restrict birth control to women of limited means by defunding Planned Parenthood add to unwanted pregnancies. Conservatives contend that choice should be made by the conservatives not by individual women with respect to abortion. The defunding of programs to help low-income women with preventative health screening increases health care costs in the future.

We see continued efforts by conservatives to reduce health care for the poor. In almost 30 states, Republican governors are refusing to expand the Medicaid coverage provided in the Affordable Healthcare Act to help millions of low income Americans to have health coverage. We see the cuts to the food stamp program, which is designed to help the poorest of the poor, as well as children and women of childbearing age. We see the refusal of the conservatives to extend unemployment benefits even though there are not enough jobs to employ the millions of people that lost their ability to make a living as a result of the near depression handed us by the conservatives and George W. Bush. We have continued resistance to provide life, liberty, and the pursuit of happiness to poor and many middle class Americans.

One of the most onerous cuts that conservatives have made in their last two budgets passed by the House of Representatives are those for food stamps (CHIP). Almost every major church in the United States has taken the position that these cuts are not justified and that they will harm the poorest of the poor including children, seniors and the disabled. One grassroots effort to try and defeat Paul Ryan's food stamp cuts is headed by Sister Simone Campbell. She is operating a thing called, "A nun on the bus." Her movement stresses that our policies must include all not just some Americans. She has been very effective in opposing the drastic spending cuts to the social network that Paul Ryan and the conservatives have championed in the House of Representatives.

It is ironic that Paul Ryan who was a Roman Catholic is insisting on cuts for the most needy in our country while proposing yet even more tax cuts for the wealthiest in America. At least on these issues Paul Ryan has made a very clear choice to put his conservative policies above the teachings of his religion.

Many of the social positions taken by conservatives express the feeling that many of these people are **on** the dole and that they really don't need the help. There is no question we have some people "game the system" and should not be receiving assistance or help at taxpayer expense. We have a responsibility as a society to both weed out those who should not be receiving help because they are capable of helping themselves while at the same time helping those that through no fault of their own need help either for an interim period or in the case of the disabled for a lifetime. Making believe that each and every person without a job can fix their problem by starting a small business or going back to school is another concept conservative push and is another broken promise to the poor in our country. These options are solutions for some but not for many unemployed.

One of the most fundamental problems and one that has a very real economic consequence is the refusal to approve an increase to the minimum wage. No one should be paid so little that even though they work they cannot afford to live on their income. That is exactly the situation millions of workers are in today with the minimum wage of $7.25 per hour.

To just offset the impact of inflation, the minimum wage should be $10.60 per hour. Thus raising the minimum wage to $10.60 is not increasing it but merely offsetting the impact of inflation. (Source www.pewresearch.org)

If we were to raise the minimum wage, we would provide millions of Americans billions of dollars more to spend which helps the economy. Every added dollar that someone making minimum wage would receive as an increase would be spent. This would be an immediately benefit the overall economy of our country. The conservative argument that small businesses cannot afford to pay higher wages is offset by the fact that many of the corporations paying minimum wage are the fast food industry and the banks that can well afford to increase the minimum wage and make less profit.

For the small businesses that simply cannot afford to pay, a reasonable wage to the workers in their company should not be in business. To continue to have a business depend on paying non-living wages so they can exist is simply not only morally wrong but is financially harming the economy of this country.

There is a concept called the "marginal propensity to consume." This is the concept that has been proven over and over again that for a lower income people the next dollar they receive will be spent. The higher your income the less of the next dollar that you receive will be spent. Thus the conservative idea of granting tax cuts to the rich means that very little if any of that additional money given to the wealthy is spent whereas help for a low income Americans by raising the minimum wage, increasing food stamps, extending unemployment or helping the disabled is immediately spent and benefits our economy.

The position taken by the conservatives on social issues has failed to deal with our country's needs in very real ways. It is difficult to argue that we should turn our backs on people who simply need help in order to survive. It is hard to justify allowing the top few percent to become more wealthy at the rate they have been and ignore the most basic needs of people that simply have no place else to turn. The concept that conservatives have that this problem should be handled by churches and charities is a copout of our responsibility as a country to help those that need help. Yes churches, and charities provide enormous benefit to people in need. However, the reality is the needs of the poor and disabled today is far greater than can be satisfied by all the churches and all the charities in our great nation. How are those with nothing to enjoy, Life, Liberty, and the pursuit of Happiness?

The resistance of the conservatives to grant the same rights to gays as to heterosexuals is also very difficult to justify. Conservatives argue we must return to the concepts of our founding fathers which include provide everyone with the ability to enjoy life, liberty, and the pursuit of happiness. Given the conservative position on gay marriage how are people, whose sexual orientation is different, to have those basic rights? It does not seem as if the conservatives really mean what they say when they claim that we should return to our roots and honor the covenants that our founding fathers intended for this country when they oppose gay marriage.

Many conservatives oppose choice for women and want to make abortion illegal. They also at the same time do not want to provide poor women with family planning and birth control. These two positions are diametrically opposed for if we provide family planning and birth control to low income women we reduce the possibility of unwanted pregnancies and abortions. Each person is entitled to his or her own opinion as to whether or not abortion should be legal. I for one do not believe it is the right alternative to be used as birth control. At the same time, the right to choose, which was granted to humankind by God is not something that the conservatives should be legislating away.

For those who are so adamantly opposed to any form of abortion I suggest that they redouble their efforts to help women with family planning and provide alternatives for unwanted pregnancy such as adoption. There is nothing wrong with trying to help women make choices that avoid abortion as a means of dealing with an unwanted pregnancy. In fact, there is everything right and moral with those efforts. However, to try to remove God given free will, as conservatives advocate, is wrong.

One of the most important issues that conservatives have staked out is the Affordable Healthcare Act and the drive to cover most Americans with health insurance. This issue certainly could be classed as a social issue but also has economic impact as well. Whether or not the dire predictions of the conservatives will materialize is yet to be determined. Certainly, by the 2016 presidential election we will have a far better idea of the overall impact that the Affordable Healthcare Act had on health coverage and health costs in the United States.

To date, some of the dire predictions of the conservatives concerning the Affordable Healthcare Act have not materialized. Conservatives promised the law would be a total failure. So far, we have seen some very real successes. We have 3 million students covered by health insurance that would not have coverage had it not been for this law. We have help for seniors to pay their prescription drug costs. We have preventive care for both seniors and women that heretofore had not been available. Restrictions have been placed on insurance companies so they cannot deny coverage because of pre-existing condition. We have ended the practice of lifetime limits as well as terminating coverage whenever an individual begins to incur large medical expenses.

The two big issues that are not clear is will we be able to cover the vast majority of those that did not have insurance prior to the Affordable Healthcare Act? Second, will health care cost be lower? To date approximately 16 million people have signed up for the coverage under the act. However unless we have significantly more people opt for coverage under the law the objective to cover 35 million Americans that did not have health insurance is still a question. By 2018, the Affordable Healthcare Act enabled the bulk of the uninsured to be covered and the law has made some inroads into reducing the health care cost spiral, we will have a huge conservative promise that was not kept. If the health care act does meet most of its objectives, the conservatives will most likely be held to account by the voters in 2020 and beyond. Given the extent, that the conservatives have gone to defeat and prevent this law from succeeding it would be difficult for voters to ignore their actions if there is a relatively high degree of success long-term of the Affordable Healthcare Act.

The Trump actions on Health Care are nothing less than criminal. His plan to replace Obamacare would have resulted in at least 13 million Americans losing their health care coverage. The added cost to lower income Americans because of reduced subsidies. The end to prevent insurance companies from refusing to cover people with pre-existing conditions, cutting benefits when claims grow and imposing lifetime caps was part of the Trump Health care plan. The insistence to repeal Obamacare without an acceptable alternative resulted in an approval of the Trump Health Care plan by the public of less than 15%. To date Donald Trump and the Republicans in Congress have done NOTHING to deal with Health Care except to weaken what remains of Obamacare.

CHAPTER 5

BROKEN PROMISES—FOREIGN POLICY AND MILITARY ISSUES

One of the major promises of the conservatives is that the use of military power, especially in the Middle East, will reduce the threat of further violence against the United States and help prevent another 9/11. Within the conservative movement is a group, which has been dubbed the neocons (Neoconservatives) who favor using our military power to deal with most trouble spots throughout the world.

After the terrorist attack on 9/11, George W. Bush and his conservative coalition invaded Afghanistan believing that the attacks from 9/11 were planned and directed by Al Qaeda utilizing Afghanistan as a home base of operation. Most Americans agreed with Bush and the conservatives that in fact it was necessary, given the horrendous attack on the United States, which we act to neutralize and punish those responsible for that unprovoked attack on our homeland. Very close to the same time, George W. Bush decided it was time to invade Iraq, which had absolutely nothing to do with 9/11 or with the Al Qaeda factions operating within Afghanistan. As a result of invading Iraq, the Afghan war was put on the back burner and was denied the necessary military assets to prosecute that war. The impact of that decision was to take a war that should have lasted two years and drag it out for almost 20 years.

We can write volumes as to the efficacy of invading Iraq. It is now clear that Bush at the time he chooses to invade Iraq had the intelligence that clearly documented the fact that Saddam Hussein had no weapons of mass destruction. In addition, a Pentagon study in December prior to the invasion determined that <u>Saddam Hussein was no military threat</u> <u>to the United States.</u> That analysis said he was only able to conduct militarily operations within the central part of Iraq itself. Despite that, George W. Bush invaded Iraq as if Iraq were a threat to the United States with the promise that he would plant the "tree of democracy" in the Middle East and reduce the threat from terrorist attacks in the future. (Source-Pentagon Assessment of Iraq Military December 2002)

More than 10 years later almost every intelligence estimate clearly shows that, the invasion of Iraq and the war in Afghanistan has not fundamentally changed the threat to our country posed by the militant Islamic factions. The conservatives will cite the fact that we have not been attacked again like we were on 9/11 as proof that their promise has been kept.

The reason we have not been attacked again is because of the defensive measures that we have taken to protect our country. The invasion of Iraq and Afghanistan created more enemies for the United States and it is believed that there is a greater risk today from attack then prior to 9/11, 2001. Therefore the conservative promise of invading Iraq and Afghanistan would significantly reduce the threat to our country in the future has simply not been achieved.

Not only has this conservative promise not been kept but the cost to our country in both human and financial resources is staggering. We had 4,488 US service personnel killed directly in Iraq. We have more than 2,000 more killed in Afghanistan. We had 32,223 troops directly injured in Iraq and that figure does not include another hundred thousand that are most likely suffered from PTSD.

The CBO has documented that we have spent directly on the wars in Iraq and Afghanistan $1.7 trillion. This figure does not include the cost of the equipment that was destroyed nor does it include the cost of the interest that this war has added to our national debt. It does not include an estimated $754 billion that we will spend through the VA over the next 30 to 40 years to deal with the injuries created in these two wars. In 2002, George W. Bush and his conservative cohorts including Dick Cheney estimated the cost of the Iraq war would be in the $50-$60 billion range. There are a number of studies that have tried to develop a comprehensively estimate of the cost of the Iraq and Afghan wars. A Brown University study estimates that the cost will be $3.2-$4 trillion. The Brookings Institute has done a study, which shows the cost could be as high as $6 trillion when you consider interest that was added to the debt, VA costs, equipment repair and replacement as well as the direct expense incurred during the fighting in Iraq and Afghanistan.

Whether you choose the $4 trillion or the $6 trillion estimate, the cost to fulfill this promise of greater stability by invading Iraq and Afghanistan is horrendous. We listen to the conservatives complain about spending and that we need to cut the budget in ways that harm poorest and most needy in our country. We can grant trillions of dollars of tax cuts to the wealthiest people in our nation while we spent $4 to 6 trillion to keep a promise that was simply not kept. After all of that, we still have factions within the conservative movement today who immediately want to use, either directly or indirectly, our military to affect change throughout the world.

Several books have been written about the hubris of the United States thinking that it can change the history of the thousand years or eliminate the animosity between religious factions and change the basic structure of governance in countries like Afghanistan, Iraq, Iran, Syria and Pakistan. The truth of the matter is we cannot materially change a thousand years of history that are responsible for the tensions that exist in the Middle East and the Muslim world. Repeating the mistakes that we made in Afghanistan and Iraq to satisfy the ill-conceived policies of the conservative neocons is unthinkable.

Just imagine what our country could have done with the $4-$6 trillion wasted on the two Bush wars. How many bridges could we have repaired? How many students could we have sent the college? How many people could we have helped refinance their mortgages, so they do not lose their homes? How long could we have extended unemployment benefits? How many people could we have fed? Every one of these alternate expenditures would have produced positive results. It would have created Jobs, reduce suffering, educated the future generation and helped millions to remain in their homes. What do we have to show from spending of $4 - $6 trillion in Iraq and Afghanistan? We have a greater risk of future terrorist attack and the death of 6,500 of our military. Is it worth another hundred thousand that will suffer for many years in the future from the physical and mental injuries incurred fighting those two wars? Although there are many that would agree that the initial attack against Afghanistan was justified when we diverted our attention to get involved with Iraq we took a war that should have lasted two years turned it into an 20-year war, the longest in our history. We could have done what was needed to be done in Afghanistan with a fraction of the cost in both dollars and lives had we not invaded Iraq. The Bush wars are one of the most reprehensible broken promises of the conservatives. We need to be very careful in the future in our use of military power to address terrorism and other areas of unrest throughout the world. A massive invasion with hundreds of thousands of troops rarely is necessary to achieve the desired result. What we are seeing today is more surgical approach whereby we try and punish or eliminate directly the elements responsible without committing huge numbers of troops for long periods of time, which cause, death, injuries and untold amount of added spending. It does not seem to matter to those that drink the conservative Kool-Aid as to the failure that is evident by our invasion of Iraq and Afghanistan. They continue to seek the use of our military in almost every conceivable situation that develops.

Trump came into office claiming within 30 days he would have a plan to destroy ISIS. In effect, what he did is continue and intensify the plan that was prepared by the Pentagon in 2014 and begun under Obama. That plan has virtually destroyed the Calafate of ISIS in Iraq. The wars in both Syria and Afghanistan are however not resolved.

Trump pulling out of the Iran Nuclear agreement developed to by the 6-nation collation with Iran threatened to destroy the secession of the nuclear program in Iran. However, what our four Western Allies and Russia did was prevent the end of the agreement by allowing Iran to sell its oil and use the banking systems. In essence, the other five countries went around Trump's withdrawal from the agreement. Time will tell if the Iran Nuclear agreement remains effective given the actions of Donald Trump's withdrawal from the agreement. In any event, the actions of Trump to withdraw, given the fact that Iran was in compliance with the terms of the Agreement, was not proper. He violated the terms of the agreement between Iran and the six countries that were party of the agreement.

CHAPTER 6

WHY MUST THE AMERICAN VOTER ABANDON THE CONSERVATIVES?

T here are two principal reasons the American voter did abandon the conservatives economic agenda beginning in 2020:

First the conservative promises have not been kept. As demonstrated in the preceding pages, with hard data and facts, what the Conservatives have promised and what they have delivered are two very different things. To continue to repeat over and over again the same conservative policies and expect a different result is clearly, as Albert Einstein said the definition of insanity.

The second reason why voters must reject the conservatives is that the vast majority of Americans simply do not support the conservative agenda to deal with the major issues that face our country. These issues are such that they must be dealt with for our country to prosper and continue to be strong both economically and militarily. If we are to deliver the promises of life, liberty, and the pursuit of happiness we must deal with things like the minimum wage, the distribution of wealth, the ability for students to obtain the education and training needed to secure employment in the 21st century, to rebuild and repair the infrastructure that is absolutely essential for both commerce and for our daily lives, to invest in research from which the new products and services of the 21st and 22nd centuries will evolve. We must balance our budget and begin repaying a debt before it destroys our economy. Simply saying NO or trying to prevent solutions to these issues is not the answer and is dangerous to the future of our country.

Let's take a look at the major issues that we face and the conservative solution to each issue:

Minimum Wage -The most recent poll shows 69% of Americans support increasing the Minimum wage. Conservatives are preventing that from taking place.

Funding Social Security - There is no question Social Security has a funding problem that must be addressed. The conservatives want to privatize Social Security that will subject it to the risks of the stock market and do absolutely nothing to deal with the funding shortfall that exists given the baby boomers over the next 50 to 60 years. As much as 80% of the American people simply do not want to privatize Social Security. Conservatives continue to try and change the very structure of Social Security even though most Republicans as well as most Americans simply do not agree with the policy.

Funding Medicare - The question of the solvency of Medicare Long-term is a given. We must find solutions to help keep the promise of health care after retirement for our American population. The conservatives want to convert the current system to a voucher plan, which provides a given amount to each senior with which they can then attempt to purchase insurance to cover their health needs during retirement. This approach would transfer the cost problem to the retired and produce hardship on millions and millions of retired Americans. Again as much as 80% of the American people do not agree with the conservative way of fixing Medicare even though they wanted it to remain solvent.

Tax cuts for the wealthiest Americans—conservatives continue to push for more and more tax cuts for the wealthiest Americans. Case in point is the last two budgets the House of Representatives passed which would lower taxes for the wealthy and aggravate the deficit. The CBO has estimated that the Ryan budgets will increase the deficit. Nevertheless, conservatives push ahead with their plans to cut help for those at the bottom and give more to those at the top. The majority of Voters believe the wealthy should pay more not less of their income in taxes.

Background checks for gun purchases—As many as 90% of Americans favor background checks before anyone can purchase a firearm. Despite this fact, conservatives have managed to block legislation that would require background checks before the purchase of firearms.

Funding cuts of social programs—Poll after poll shows that most Americans do not want to turn their backs on the poor, disabled or the unemployed. At the same time, most taxpayers do not want to support people who are able to work. However, the slash and burn approach taken by the conservatives is not acceptable to the majority of Americans. A very real inconsistency in the conservative policy of cutting the budget and reducing fraud is they have cut auditors needed to help control fraud. The spending cuts that began in 2011 have reduced the number of auditors in all agencies of the federal government. You do not lower fraud by cutting those charged with preventing fraud! (Source AP 4/13/2014)

Tax Reform - There is a lot of complaining about our income tax system but no action to reform it. The law is full of loopholes that are designed to reduce or eliminate taxes for the very wealthy. The Bush tax cuts lowered the tax rates mostly for wealthier individuals. He kept the loopholes that enable people like Mitt Romney to only pay 14% tax in federal income tax while his secretary pays 25% tax. We constantly hear the conservatives complain about high taxes in the United States. The truth is taxes are at an 80 year low. Tax Freedom Day, which is intended to measure the date when we finish paying all taxes—federal, state and local for the year has gone from May 1, in 2000 to April 21st in 2014. That clearly demonstrating that the total tax burden in the United States has dropped since 2000. (Source-www.taxfoundatiion.org).

When we look at our tax burden compared with the other industrialized nations, we find the United States ranks third from the bottom. In a 2010 study done by the Organization of Economic Cooperation and Development (OECD) found the United States had a total tax burden federal, state and local of 24.5% of GDP. This compares with 40 to 45% of GDP in most of the European countries. We need to enact legislation that requires all Presidential, vice presidential and gubernatorial candidates to make their income taxes public for 10 years prior to the time they run for office.

The CBO reported that the tax burden from just the federal income tax was at 21% of GDP in 2000 when we had a balanced budget. In 2013, the federal income tax is 15.5% of GDP. The impact of reducing the income tax revenue from 21% of GDP to 15.5% of GDP is more than an $800 billion per year loss in revenue. When you add the lost revenue because of the loopholes and the tax cheats there is no doubt why this country is running a budget deficit. The Trump Tax Cut of 2017 will further reduce the revenue loss and the present of GDP of Federal Income Taxes.

Immigration reform - The majority of Americans do not want to deport 11 million people who have not entered our country legally. Most Americans recognize that there needs to be a solution to this problem and that there should be some mechanism for those who want to remain here to do so legally. However, here again even though we have had a comprehensive measure to deal with immigration pass the Senate, conservatives in the House refuse to allow this bill to come to a vote. Most Americans do not support what the conservatives are doing by only allowing bills to come to a vote when Republicans believe they have the votes to get their way on a Bill. Nor do most people support the conservative tactic of using the filibuster in the Senate to again prevent a vote. The filibuster has been used over 450 times since President Obama took office. Preventing a vote in either the House or the Senate does not allow either chamber to function as the Constitution intended. The purpose of these two parts of the legislative branch was to vote and render their decision on proposed legislation. When conservatives prevent a vote, they shelter their members from going on record to either support or oppose the measure in question. This shelters the Congressperson or Senator from the scrutiny of the electorate.

Rebuilding the infrastructure—Despite the fact that everyone understands we need safe highways, bridges and dams as well as an effective electrical grid the conservatives have repeatedly prevented the repair and maintenance of these essential elements. Two years ago, President Obama proposed a Bill to help create jobs and rebuild our infrastructure. Even if we did not need the jobs that the infrastructure repair will create, the fact of the matter is for both our business and personal use we must have a viable infrastructure. All the estimates that the engineers have made document that we have trillions of dollars in needed repairs that are not being done because the conservatives will not approve the spending. In addition, the loss in Federal Income taxes from the 2017 Tax Cut make the funding to repair the infrastructure repair more impossible. The Federal gas tax revenue has been falling due to the increase in vehicle fuel-efficiency. Add to this the increase in the cost of asphalt as well as road construction and the result is the Highway Trust Fund will be insolvent by October 1, 2014 unless Congress acts.

Conservatives have blocked added funding for highway construction and have no answers when bridges and other infrastructure fail.

We need to change the gasoline tax system from a fixed per gallon tax to one that is adjusted each year for increased road construction costs and fuel-efficiency growth.

Our parents and grandparents spent the money to build the infrastructure so that we could prosper as a nation. The conservatives simply ignore the fact that our bridges, dams, and roads are getting older and must be repaired. We need to obtain the resources needed to make these repairs by having the wealthy in our country pay more in taxes. We simply cannot afford to make the necessary repairs and add it to the national debt.

The United States is at a crossroads. We cannot simply ignore the major issues we face because of their magnitude and impact on our country and each of our lives. When you look at the conservative agenda, you will see it has either created the problem or enabled the problem to develop. Two of the best examples of this are the increase in the National Debt from $900 billion in 1980 to $25 trillion in 2020. The tax and spend policies of Reagan, George W. Bush, Trump and the impact of the corona virus are responsible for most of the increase the national debt. Most recently, we started with a balanced budget (2000), reduced the federal revenue by 30% with the Bush tax cuts, and then increase spending by 10% to pay the added cost of two Bush wars. The result was a huge deficit. This is precisely what we did in 2001–2003 despite the fact that the very same conservative policy, employed in 1981, produced the very same increase in the deficit.

The common thread that runs through the conservative agenda is repeated repeatedly. Conservatives ignore the facts to justify an ideology that simply does not work. Everything from the budget to global warming demonstrates the fact that conservatives are more like religious zealots then informed people.

We have 98% of world scientists acknowledge that global warming is taking place. They have measured the increase in ocean temperature. They have documented that the level of the oceans has risen approximately a foot. We have satellite images that prove the polar caps are melting and we measured the increased acidity of the ocean from the carbon dioxide that we are putting into the atmosphere by burning fossil fuels. Increasing the Ph. of the oceans is killing the coral and many types of marine life TODAY. Despite all of this, we have some conservatives that will not even acknowledge there is global warming.

The comments made by Senator Marco Rubio Sunday May 11th on ABC's *This Week* are a perfect example of conservatives ignoring reality. Senator Rubio said "I don't agree with the notion that some are putting out there, including scientists, that somehow there are actions we can take today that would actually have an impact on what's happening in our climate" He then blasted President Obama as "Commander-in- chief, not a meteorologist." What credentials does Senator Rubio have as a meteorologist? He went on to say, "And I do not believe the laws (scientists) propose will pass will do anything about it, except it will destroy our economy." What does Senator Rubio think losing the Gulf, Boston, New York or most of the coastal areas of Florida would do to our economy?

It may be that global warming would occur even without the untold amounts of CO2 we are putting into the atmosphere but the issue is we are probably accelerating the global warming process. However, to deny that global warming is even taking place and do nothing is risking a global catastrophe.

Our country needs to totally reverse what began in 1981 and reemerged in 2001. If we are to prosper and hand our sons, daughters, and grandchildren a vibrant free nation we need to resolve the issues we face. It is time to rebuild and repair our infrastructure. It is time to invest in basic research. It is time to make sure that every student is able to get the education and training necessary so that they can be productive members of society. We need to balance our budget and begin paying down the huge debt before the interest on that debt buries us all. We need to look at the changing atmospheric conditions in our world and see what we can do either to slow the progress or to provide some defensive mechanisms to protect us from the rising oceans. We need to deal with the funding issues that jeopardize Social Security and Medicare. We need to get a handle on the ever-increasing costs of healthcare. We need to do a better job at increasing the minimum wage, streamline our welfare systems to help those that needed help and deny help to those who would abuse it.

All of this is going to take a joint effort between government and the private sector. We must have effective regulation and honestly look at our country and the reasons why we have the major problems that we have today. The biggest problem with the conservatives is that they are not interested in WHY things happened because when they look at the WHY, they find that it comes directly into conflict with their philosophy and the policies. No place is this more clear than in what caused the deficit to rise or what caused the Great Depression and a near depression 2008. We need to have those with the resources pay more of their income not to punish the wealthy but because we need the money. We need the added money to balance our budget and make the investments in our country that are absolutely essential to ensure our future welfare.

The American people do not want to repeat the suffering that our parents and grandparents endured in the 1929—38. Americans want to avoid the misery we endured because of the recession of 2007-2008. The voters of this country need to recognize that the conservative agenda has not kept its promise. The conservative agenda is primarily responsible for the deficit as well as allowing business to act without restraint, which resulted in the Great Depression and the near depression that came to a head in 2008. For anyone that would like to relive these difficult periods, I suggest they support the conservatives. For any American that wants to avoid another Great Depression or the economic crisis we lived through in 2008, it is time to remove the conservatives from a position of power in the House, Senate and keep them out of the White House. If the Democrats are unable to control 60 votes in the Senate but get control of the House and White House, they will need to again change the Senate Rules to either make a filibuster a true filibuster by requiring the Senator to speak on the subject or by requiring only 51 votes to bring a bill to a vote in the Senate.

For any voter who is still undecided as to whether or not the conservatives deserve to remain in any position of power within the federal government consider the following. We were promised that the Iraq war would be quick, remember the "Shock and Awe," and would cost $50 to $60 billion. The Iraq and Afghan wars cost this country somewhere between $4 and $6 Trillion and lasted 11 years. In 1980, Ronald Reagan promised that if we reduce taxes for the wealthy we would balance the budget and the benefits would trickle-down to the middle class. George W. Bush made the same promise in 2001. The bottom line is the wealth in our country is far more concentrated at the top then it has never been in the past. Middle income Americans are struggling to simply live. We have created a mountain of debt. The promises of Ronald Reagan and George W. Bush were not kept. Their conservative agenda has added $31 trillion to the National Debt. That means each year the American taxpayer is paying between $660 and $825 billion in interest to service the increase in the debt caused by the broken conservative promises.

What is even more disturbing is what we did with that $31 Trillion dollars since 1981? Approximately $2 trillion was used to fight the Bush wars. The remaining $29 trillion was used to pay for the day-to-day operating costs of the United States. We did not use it to build roads, build bridges or educate our children. It was not paid to retirees for Social Security or Medicare. None of this money was used to invest in long-term infrastructure that would benefit us in the future. It would be as if in your home budget you borrowed 30% of the amount that you spent every month on food, clothing, utilities and things to simply live.

In 2016, our country again allowed the Conservatives and Donald J. Trump to continue the destructive policies that took place under both Ronald Reagan and George W. Bush. By about 80,000 votes in three states despite the loss in the popular vote of over 3 Million votes, Trump won the Electoral College and became the 45th President of the United States. To compound this mistake, the Republicans remained in control of both the House of Representatives and the Senate. All the polls clearly showed that the Republicans and Donald Trump only had the approval of about 35% of the Voters. This happened because 45 % (106,163,000) of Voting Age Americans did not vote.

The continuation of the Conservative agenda despite the promises of Trump and the Republicans that the results would be different so far are proving the famous statement of Albert Einstein to be true, "Doing the same thing over and over again expecting a different result is insanity."

Despite the fact that Trump and the Republicans had only the support of about 35% of Americans, they have continued the same Conservative policies that broke the Promises when tried by Ronald Reagan and George W. Bush.

The tax cuts so far have not benefitted the middle class to any great extent. In fact, the elimination of the Personal Exemption for families with two or more children will see their taxes increase starting in 2018. The benefits from the Trump/Republican Tax Cut are going to people with incomes over $200,000 per year and Big Business. There is no Trickle down and Business is not using their tax cuts to grow their business, increase wages for their workers or create living wage jobs. Rather they are using the tax cuts to buy back their own stock to help drive up the price on the Stock market.

The promise to increase GDP growth from about 2% per year to between 4 to 5% has not happened. The GDP growth rate for the first quarter of 2018 stood at 2.2%. Most economists believe the sustained growth rate in GDP will be far less than the 4-5% promised by

Donald Trump. After the corona virus, the GDP is expected to be -5.5% to -7.5%.

The promised growth in the economy is not making up for the lost revenue from the tax cut and the Annual Budget Deficit is up $400 Billion Dollars or 80% increase in FY 2019 before the corona virus.

The Republicans and Trump have weakened regulations on banks and consumer lending companies, which puts consumers at greater risk. Trump has increased the interest rates on some Student Loans. The spending cuts for food, housing, heating assistance and Medicaid is harming the poorest of the poor.

The immigration policies and the forced separation of children from their parents that Trump and his Attorney General have started with their "Zero Tolerance Policy" is an inhumane outrage.

Trump is weakening our relationship with Canada, Mexico and our European Allies while at the same time promoting Dictatorships like North Korea, Russia and China.

Trump is imposing tariffs on our Allies and China, which risks a trade war, higher prices for imported goods and retaliation against American Agricultural and manufactured goods.

Donald Trump's attacks on our Constitution and the agencies that protect our system of government is dangerous. His contention that he has the absolute right to Pardon Himself amounts to Sovern Immunity a practice that ended with the kings in Europe in the 1200 hundreds. His attacks on the Department of Justice and the FBI. His attacks on Judges that render rulings he does not agree with or are against him personally like the Trump University Lawsuit. Trump's contention the Free Press, which is guaranteed by the First Amendment, is according to Donald Trump, **"is one of our greatest dangers."** His attempt to obstruct justice by firing the FBI Director when he refused to end the General Flynn investigation and pledge loyalty to Donald Trump rather than the law and Constitution. His attempt on four occasions to get the Attorney General to reverse his recusal from supervising the Robert Mueller investigation of the Trump Campaign and the actions of the Russians to help Donald Trump win the Presidency because of the conflict of interest the Attorney general had as being part of the Trump Campaign.

Despite the clear and present danger posed to our Constitution by these actions of Donald Trump, the Republicans in Congress are not exercising their responsibilities under the Separation of Powers to act to impeach the President. They are allowing him to abuse and exceed the power granted him under our Constitution. In essence, Congress is failing to meet its responsibilities under the Constitution.

At this point, the only component of our government that is acting in agreement with the law and Constitution are the Courts. Given the refusal of the Republicans in Congress to act, only the voters have the power to ensure the United States remains true to the principals established by our Founding Fathers in 1789. If the 2/3 of Americans who do not agree with or Support what Donald Trump and the Republicans are doing better VOTE to support our Republic on November 3, 2020. ANYONE WHO WANTS AMERICA TO REMAIN GREAT MUST END THE CONTROL OF THE GOVERNMENT BY DONALD J. TRUMP AND REPUBLICANS IN NOVEMBER 2020!

CHAPTER 7

SUMMARY

W e are seeing yet another example of the most fundamental precepts of the Conservative Agenda break the promises made to support its adoption by Donald Trump and the Republican Controlled Congress in 2017. We have watched a skillful **"carnival barker"** convinced some American Voters that he will be able to do things that prior administrations had not been able to deliver. In other cases, Donald Trump has made promises that are ill conceived and are not in the best long-term interest of the United States. In addition, we have a President who continually Lies, makes up things and presents them as facts or distorts information to create LIES! Presidents in the past have lied to the American People. We had Ronald Reagan and Iran Contra. We had Bill Clinton and Monica Lewinsky. We had George W. Bush and the Weapons of Mass Destruction in Iraq. We had Barrack Obama and you can keep your Doctor. However NEVER have we had a President lie from his second day in Office and almost every day thereafter.

On January 21, 2017, Donald Trump started lying as President by claiming his inauguration crowd was bigger than Barrack Obama's eight year earlier. Despite the pictures taken on both inauguration days by the National Park Service showing this was a lie. Donald Trump doubled down and demanded the National Park Service to review the crowd size. The first explanation was the picture taken of the Trump Crowd was not taken until 1:25 pm after many people had departed while the picture at Obama's inauguration was taken at noon. The time stamps on the National Park Service Pictures clearly prove this claim was another lie. The time stamp on the Trump Picture was 12:01pm and the time stamp on the Obama Picture was 12:07 pm. The review of the crowd size demanded by Donald Trump by the Park Service confirmed that the crowd at the Obama inauguration on January 20, 2009 was in fact larger than the crowd at the Trump inauguration on January 20, 2017. In fact the difference in the crowd size was significant and the New York Times said the Trump Crowd was about 1/3 the size of the Obama crowd. Despite the irrefutable difference shown in the side-by-side pictures, Donald Trump persisted in this lie to satisfy his Ego, sent his new Press Secretary, Sean Spicer out to announce this lie, and destroyed Mr. Spicer's credibility with the American People.

Almost every day after January 21st 2017, Donald Trump has lied or made misleading statements. The Washington Post's Fact Checker identified over 3,000 untrue or misleading statements made by Donald J. Trump in his first 466 days in office. His lies covered almost every possible subject and in many cases were about very significant issues facing America and the world. Although other Presidents have lied or mislead the American People in the past, there has never been anything like the number and breath of lies told by any other President of the United States! In addition to the obvious failure in the Moral leadership of Donald Trump's lying, if we come to a point where a serious issue arises, Americans and many of our allies may not believe the President of the United States. That holds the potential for worldwide disaster.

The results so far from the Conservative agenda that is being implemented by Donald Trump and the Republican Controlled Congress shows the very same failures we saw during the Reagan and Bush 43 administrations. The updated statistics show the downside of ending regulation of banks and financial institutions on the average American. Higher fees less protection and a return to the excesses that helped bring on the "Near Depression of 2008." We see a spike in the Annual Budget Deficit from less than $600 Billion to $1 Trillion Dollars, which is an increase of 80%. We are not seeing the promised Business invest and creation of living wage jobs or to increase the wages of their workers in any meaningful amount. A few companies have granted small one-time payments but there has not been any substantial wage increases to workers. Average weekly wage increased a modest 2.7% under Trump. GDP Growth in the first quarter of 2018 is 2.2% nothing like the 4 to 5 % promised by Donald Trump. We are seeing Big Business use the windfall from the tax cut to buy back their own stock to benefit the owners. By the end of 2019, companies have purchased almost $500 Billion Dollars of their stock with the business tax cuts.

At this point a review of the ten top promises made by Donald Trump during the 2016 Presidential Campaign should be remembered:

1. Build a Wall along our southern Border and make Mexico pay for the cost. (This promise violates the open and welcoming policy toward Immigrants that helped make us GREAT. It ignores the fact that a Wall will not fix the problems with our Immigration system. It also ignores that such a Wall or Fence cannot be built without the Federal Government acquiring the right-of-way along its 2000-mile length. It also ignored the very explicit statement by Mexico that they do not want a Wall and WOULD NOT PAY FOR THE WALL!)

2. Ban Muslims from entry into the United States on a temporary basis. (This promise was upheld by the Supreme Court on June 26, 2018 in a 5 to 4 decision).

3. Bring Manufacturing Jobs Back to the United States. (This promise is only possible to a very limited extent and only in certain industries. It is a promise that ignores the understanding

of why manufacturing jobs have been lost. The most fundamental reason for lost manufacturing jobs is automation. The second reason in importance is the cheaper labor costs in many countries compared with wages in the United States.)

4. Impose Tariffs on goods made in China, Canada, The EU and Mexico. (This promise shows a lack of understanding how protectionist policies impact our economy. First tariffs increase the price to American Consumers for any goods the Tariff are imposed upon. It most often results in retaliatory Tariffs against goods made in the United States, which adversely impact Jobs and the profits of American Companies and risks a Trade War in which EVERYONE LOOSES. There are other ways to impact a trade imbalance of specific goods i.e. Steel or Aluminum such as imposing Import Quotas and an even less intrusive option is to provide government subsidies to companies that are endangered. Our protectionist trade policy in the 1920's was an important component, along with uncontrolled speculation in the Stock Market, which caused the Great Depression in 1929. In addition to the dangers posed by a Trade War, the countries that Donald Trump is attacking with his Tariffs hold large amounts of U.S. Debt. If these countries would choose and retaliate by either selling debt, they currently hold, which could drive up the cost of U.S. debt, or refuse to purchase new U.S. Debt that could make it hard or more costly to finance the one Trillion Dollars we are adding each year to our National Debt. As of March 2018, the countries who Trump is attacking with Tariffs hold the following amount of U.S. Debt, in billions of U.S. Dollars:

China 1187.7 France 80.0
UK 263.7 Germany 76.5
Canada 92.9 Mexico 45.2
Source. U.S Treasury Department).

5. Change or withdraw from NAFTA and the Trans-Pacific Trade Partnerships. (Renegotiating trade agreements that may have provisions with negative consequences on the U.S. Trade is a wise policy but unilaterally withdrawing from such agreements is destructive and risks either being isolated or triggering a trade war.)

6. Repeal Obamacare and replace with Market-Based System. (Repealing Obamacare before there was a viable alternative would make health care worse and result in millions of Americans with NO COVERAGE. It also ignores that the system prior to Obamacare for people under 65 was a Market-Based health care system and it failed to meet the health care needs of over 30 million Americans.)

7. Renegotiate the Iran Nuclear Deal. (Attempting to renegotiate any agreement that has flaws or omissions is a sound idea. Simply abandoning the agreement and wind up with NO AGREEMENT demonstrates the incompetence of the party pulling out of the agreement.)

8. Leave Social Security as is. (This is a position that more than 80% of Americans support. They want the promises made under Social Security Kept and do not support changing the system. In order to accomplish this, the revenue coming into the system must be increased. The Baby-Boomers have altered the demographics of the System and changed from 5 or more working and paying into the system for every person drawing retirement benefits to more like 2 working for everyone receiving retirement benefits. The refusal to increase Social Security payroll taxes will prevent this promise from being kept!)

9. Cut Taxes. (Given the fact, we continue to have an Annual Budget Deficit that adds to the overall National Debt, which has reached over $31 Trillion in 2023, and the need to rebuild our infrastructure and military we need MORE not LESS tax revenue. The tax cut was the WRONG POLICY GIVEN OUR

NEEDS. We must invest in our country and that will require higher taxes be paid by upper income Americans to pay for what is needed!)
10. Bomb and/or take the oil from ISIS. (First, the Oil does not belong to ISIS. It is against international law to take the oil from the country in which it is located. Finally, simply bombing ISIS will not end their existence or the danger they present.)

DONALD TRUMP MOVING FORWARD

Donald Trump spent his entire business career and time on his TV show The Apprentice calling the shots. In essence he ran his companies like Dictatorships. His approach was "Do it my way or Your Fired." With the release of his tax Returns we have learned that Trump's approach to running his numerous business enterprises was an unmitigated disaster. Not only did many of his individual ventures fail but he incurred some of the largest losses ever seen by a businessman. In addition, he does not understand or care about the Separation Powers that is the foundation of our system of government established by the U. S. Constitution in 1789.

He seeks personal loyalty not loyalty to the Law and Constitution. He attacks anything that does not conform to what he wants to be done. The FBI, Department of Justice, the Courts and the Free Press. Donald Trump's statement that, **The Free Press is "the enemy of the people"** is the ultimate proof of Donald Trump's distain for our system of government. Demanding personal loyalty, attacking the courts and the press was used by Hitler usurp power in Germany.

Another tactic used by Hitler to garner support was to tell lies over and over again until many people believed the LIES AS TRUTH. The Washington Post Fact Checker documented over 30,000 false or misleading statements made by Donald Trump during his four years as President. Other fact checkers such as FactCheck.org and PolitiFact.org also documents many thousands of Trump lies during his four years in office. All politicians lie at times but Donald Trump took lying to an "Art Form" and he lied or made misleading statements constantly.

The Trump lies started during his second day in office. He claimed that the size of his Inauguration crowd was larger than Obama's in 2009. When the side by side pictures of the Obama and Trump crowds were shown, the Trump claim was shown to be a lie. The size of the Obama crowd was significantly larger then the Trump crowd. He could not accept the reality shown by the pictures so Donald Trump personally pressured the National Park Service to Crop the picture of his crown to show only the area where his supporters could be seen. The back section of the ellipse which was packed with Obama supporters in 2009 was almost empty of Trump supporters in 2017.

The most disturbing lies are about him winning the 2020 Presidential election. From election-day on, he said the election was stolen and that he was elected President. The Lie of the BIG STEAL was repeated over and over again by him and his

supporters. Donald Trump demanded recount
after recount and in every one the results were the
same - Trump Lost! He had his lawyers go into
State and Federal courts asserting that the election
was rigged and the results should be set aside. His
lawyers filed 62 lawsuits and in every case the
courts, including two cases that reached the
Supreme Court, rejected his assertions for lack of
evidence. Some of the Judges described the Trump
lawsuits as, "frivolous."

He has created a Cult, where the loyalty is to
Donald Trump just like to Adolf Hitler in
Germany beginning in 1932. Despite Donald
Trump's blatant violation of the most basic
elements of the U.S. Constitution, the Republican
controlled Congress has refused to impeach him as
provided in Article II, Section 4 of the
Constitution. Many of his supporters include the
American White Nationalist Movement consisting
of ultra-right Neo-Nazi, Neo-Fascist, and White
Supremacist and Ku Klux Klan members. Trumps
statements at a news conference on August 15,
2017 about the violent demonstrations of White-
Supremacists in Charlottesville when he said, "You
also had people that were very fine people, on both
sides" show his support for these groups. During a
Presidential debate on September 30, 2020 Trump
was pressed by the moderator, Chris Wallace to
disavow white-supremacists. He would not directly
do so and made his this statement, "Proud Boys
(one of these groups) Stand Back and Stand By.
But I'll tell you what: somebodies got to do
something about Antifa and the left." The
definition of Antifa is a group of militant groups

that oppose Fascism and other extreme right-wing ideology.

The House brought the first Impeachment charges against Donald Trump on December 18, 2019 for Abuse of Power and Obstruction of Congress. The second articles of Impeachment were brought against Trump on January 11, 2021 for Incitement of Insurrection for the attack on the Capitol January 6, 2021. BOTH TIMES every Republican in the Senate announced, before they saw the evidence, they would not vote to remove him from office. The only recourse was for the Voters to remove the control of Congress from the Republicans which they did on November 3, 2020. In November 2022 Republicans managed to regain control in the House with a very slim majority and a group of some of the most radical people in our country.

Many Americans mistakenly believe with the election of Joe Biden and the repudiation of Donald Trump on November 3, 2020 with a popular vote loss of over 7 million votes our Republic is secure. Republican leaders like former VP Mike Pence urge us to move on and forget the past actions of former President Donald Trump. That advice flies in the face of the Judicial System we have followed since our founding. When someone violates our laws, especially serious felonies, we do not just "move on". We investigate their actions and if a Grand Jury and prosecutor find sufficient evidence, the person is charged and brought to trial. If we were to accept the advice of the Republican leadership, we would need to empty all our prisons.

Donald Trump must be treated like any other
citizen who act in ways that appear to violate
the law. We do not have a King or Sovern and
to simply "move on" and not follow the same
process for Donald Trump as for all other
citizens would violate a bedrock component of
our legal system - Equal Treatment Under the
Law. He must be held to account for his actions
associated with the following possible felonies:

The January 6th attack on the Capitol and
Congress. Of all the potential offenses Donald
Trump engaged in before, during and after his
term as President, nothing comes close to the
serious nature of his attempting to overturn the
2020 election and stop the peaceful transfer of
power. The January 6th House Select Committee
concluded, Donald Trump planned and
encouraged the attack on the Capitol and
threatened the lives of the VP, Speaker of the
House and members of Congress on January 6,
2021 when his supporters rioted at the Capitol.
On December 22, 2022 the January 6th House
Committee unanimously recommending that
Donald Trump be charged with the following
felonies:

>Obstruction of an official proceeding
>Conspiracy to defraud the Unites States
>Conspiracy to make a false statement
>Insurrection

>(Note the DOJ and Special Counsel
>requested and received the evidence from the
>January 6th House Committee including the
>sworn testimony)

The January 6th House Select Committee was a
bipartisan committee consisting of 7 Democrats
and 2 Republicans. Three other Republicans
were to be part of the committee but were
prevented from serving on the committee by the
GOP Minority Leader of the House
Republicans, Keven McCarthy. The committee
was chaired by Bennie Thompson (D) and the
Vice Chair was Liz Cheney (R).

The Committee worked for 18 months. They
released an executive summary totaling 154
pages the final report was 845 pages long. They
conducted more than 1000 interviews including
from Trump's closest advisors. The supporting
documents include sworn statements, exhibits,
videos, emails, text messages, letters, power
point presentations made by the White House.
The amount of supporting evidence is enormous.

Some of the most important evidence
documents the January 6th attack on the Capitol
was planned starting in mid-December to
include a Trump team command center in the
Willard Hotel located near the White House.
Authorities found guns, knives, bombs and Bear
spray to support the insurrection at the Capitol
January 6, 2021.

The January 6th insurrection would not have
taken place without the involvement of Donald
Trump and his call for his right-wing extremist
groups to come to the Washington and march
on the Capitol January 6th.

Donald Trump used the lie the election was stolen (The Big Steal) to garnish support from the extremists groups that attacked the Capitol and Congress on January 6th. The evidence presented by numerous top advisors was that Trump was told he lost the election. They included his AG, Bill Bar who told Trump "The claims of (voter) fraud were bullshit". Likewise his Chief of Staff, Campaign Advisor, White House council as well as his Daughter Ivanka Trump told him he lost the election. Despite this, Trump listened to people like Rudy Giuliani, Steve Bannon and Stephen Miller.

The evidence provided under oath to the January 6th House Select Committee by Cassidy Hutchinson, the Assistant to the Chief of Staff, Mark Meadows was among the most damaging. Most of her testimony was corroborated by the testimony of other White House staff. She testified that her boss told her on November 18, 2020 that Trump, "has pretty much acknowledged that he lost," Despite that Trump, to this day, asserts he won the 2020 election. Ms. Hutchinson also testified about being told by Tony Ornato, Dep. Chief of Staff that Trump demanded the Secret Service take him to the Capitol while his supporters were rioting on January 6, 2021 and that the conversation was very heated. Trump told the driver that, "he was the f****** President and wanted to go to the Capitol." Later Mr. Ornato testified he did not recall telling Ms. Hutchinson about that incident but another White House staff member confirmed hearing him tell that story to Ms. Hutchinson.

Ms. Hutchinson also testified that she saw Donald Trump in the small White House dining room watching the riot by his followers at the Capitol in January 6th. Other staff members also testified about Trump watching the rioters on TV for over three hours. Ms. Hutchinson testified Trump seemed pleased and in support of what was taking place. This was confirmed by other members of the White House staff in the room with Trump. Even though Trump had command of 10,000 Washington National Guard troops several blocks from the Capitol, he refused to act despite a frantic call from Kevin McCarthy and urging by Mark Meadows. He also refused to go on TV and urge the rioters to end the carnage for more than three hours.

The time line on January 6th is very telling. At 12 noon Trump made his speech at his Save America Rally. At that speech he said, "We will never give up, We will never concede." "Mike Pence, I hope you're going to stand up for the good of the Constitution and for the good of our country." Even before his speech ended, his followers were massing at the steps of the Capitol. About the same time VP Pence released a statement saying, his role in the certification of the electoral votes was "largely ceremonial" and saying he could not reject some of the electoral vote as Trump demanded. The inaction of Donald J. Trump on January 6, 2021, as his supporters were attacking our

Capitol for the first time since British attack in 1814, make Benedict Arnold look like a Patriot. January 6th was caused by the Fake claims by Donald Trump. His denial of the 2020 Presidential election results and Far-right extremism.

The evidence amassed by the January 6th Committee proves the objective of the January 6th insurrection at the Capitol was to disrupt the Certification of President Elect Joseph R. Biden as the 46th President of the United States and to prevent the peaceful transfer of power on January 20, 2021. No action is more serious then what took place on that day!

A December 2020 report from Berkeley Research Group, a firm that Donald Trump hired to provide support for his assertions of the voter fraud, was uncovered. That report says there was no evidence of voter fraud in the six key states they were hired to study. Trump received that report at the end of December 2020 and kept it hidden. Thus when Donald Trump told his followers on January 6, 2021 that the election was stolen, he knew that was a lie. That lie and his direction to march to the Capitol and "Fight like Hell" resulted in the insurrection on that dreadful day.

Source: CNN

In addition to the actions of Donald Trump in the January 6th Insurrection, there are numerous other investigations about possible criminal activities of the 45th President, before, during and after he was President.

Maintaining two sets of property valuations on the same properties- The low values to reduce tax liability and the inflated values to obtain larger bank loans violate Tax and Banking laws. His tax document show for 40 Wall Street and The Trump International Hotel and Tower show different values for NYC taxes and lenders. They are low for NYC Taxes and high when he wanted to obtain a loan.

Source: Daily Mail by James Gordon

Attempting to change the results of the election in Georgia by pressuring the Secretary of State Brad Raffensperger (R) to create 11,780 fake votes. A 23 member Grand Jury in Fulton County Georgia is deciding if Donald Trump and others committed crimes in their attempt to illegally overturn the entire 2020 election in Georgia. The Grand Jury submitted their findings to the Fulton County District Attorney, Fanti T. Willis who will decide if charges will be brought against Donald Trump. Conviction could result in Donald Trump serving prison time in Georgia.

Source: The Guardian by Chris McGreal

Trump and his allies created fraudulent certifications of ascertainment that falsely asserted Trump won the Electoral College vote in seven key states. The theory put forth by John Eastman in his memos claimed the Vice President could swap out the actual electors for alternate electors. The Constitution grants NO SUCH AUTHORITY to the Vice President.

Trumps personal lawyer, Rudy Giuliani coordinated this scheme across the seven states.

Source: Wikipedia.

Documents that by law are required to be given The National Archives which included Classified Documents containing the highest classification were found at Trump's home in Florida. These documents were not properly secured and Trump ignored subpoenas to return the classified documents. His lawyer lied about returning classified documents as directed by the court.

At the beginning of May 2021, The National Archives (NARA) was concerned Trump took records from the White House when he left office January 20, 2021 and they requested the documents from Trump on May 6, 2021. The NARA continued requesting the return of the documents from Trump and in December 2021 Trump officials informed NARA they found 12 boxes of records.

On January 18, 2022 15 Boxes of Presidential records that had been stored at Mar-a-Lago were returned to the Archives. It was discovered these boxes contained classified documents and were mixed with other documents. A total of 184 classified documents were discovered of which 25 were Top Secret, 92 Secret and 67 confidential.

In February the DOJ requested the FBI to open a criminal investigation into this matter. On

February 18, the NARA notified the Congressional Oversite Committee that classified documents were found in the 14 or the 15 boxes of records recovered from Trump's home in Florida. On May 11 the DOJ issued a subpoena for any additional records. On June 3, FBI and DOJ attorney were given envelope that contained 38 classified documents including 17 marked Top Secret. The DOJ was given a signed certification saying a diligent search had been completed and no more classified documents remained.

On August 5th the DOJ requested a search warrant of Trump's home predicated on information from an insider at Mar-a-Lago that additional classified documents remained at Trump's resort. On August 8th a search was conducted at Trump's home and more than 100 additional classified documents were found some of which were totally unsecured in Trump's bedroom and desk.

Trump first claimed the FBI had planted the records at Mar-a-Logo. Then he claimed he had declassified the records. He asserted the records he took from the White House were his property despite the Presidential Records Act that clearly states all records belong to the National Archives. The outcome of the investigation of the Special Council, Jack Smith could result in criminal charges against trump for taking the records, refusing to return them as well as improper storage.

Source: AP

The evidence surrounding each of the above must be considered by state and federal officials, and if the evidence shows likely violation of the law, Donald J. Trump must be charged and made to stand trial. The danger to our Republic of ignoring the actions of Donald Trump undermines our system of Justice.

In addition, Donald J. Trump must be held to account for his actions to deter ANY future President from committing similar offenses.

In January 2023 it was revealed that, Classified Documents have been discovered at the homes of President Biden, from when he was Vice President and former Vice President Pence. Although these two cases do not appear to be intentional, we clearly have a major problem about how classified documents are handled by the most senior members of our government as the leave office. To protect our countries secrets, this must be addressed as soon as possible!

Even more troubling was the discovery in February 2023 that 100 Top Secret Documents were scanned and downloaded on Donald Trump's Laptop.

How Democrats are enacting laws to improve the economy, address our long term needs and help the vast majority of Americans live a better life.

2021:

American Rescue Plan - $1.9 Trillion dollar recovery plan was signed into law March 11, 2021 to deal with the impact on Coved

19 on individuals and small business. More than 12 million jobs and millions of small business were created in the two years since its passage. All GOP members in the House and Senate voted NO on this Bill.

Infrastructure Investment and Jobs Act - $1.2 Trillion dollar 10 year plan was signed into law November 15, 2021 for roads and Bridge rebuilding, broadband expansion, Electric car recharging stations, clean water, improved transportation and upgrade airports, clean energy, harden infrastructure from damage by extreme weather and cleaning up industrial and energy sites. Only 19 GOP Senators and 13 GOP House members supported this Bill.

Increased Debt Limit - $2.5 Trillion was signed into law December 16. 2021 for added borrowing to 2023.
Only 1 GOP House member and NO GOP Senator supported this Bill.

Juneteenth National Holliday - Recognize the day we ended slavery was signed into law June 17, 2021.
Only Fourteen GOP House members voted against this Bill and all GOP Senators supported this Bill.

Uyghur Forced Labor Prevention Act – Stop importation of goods made in China that employed forced labor was signed into law December 23, 2021. All but 1 GOP House member and all GOP Senators supported this Bill.

2022:

Bipartisan Gun Safety Bill - Signed into law June 25, 2022 provides funding to help implement Red Flag Laws and restrict individuals involved with domestic violence from having guns. Also provides mental health funding. Does not include many of the urgently needed restrictions to ban assault weapons or mandatory background checks to purchase guns. Only 15 GOP Senators and 14 GOP House members voted YES for this bill.

CHIPS and Science Act - $280 Billion dollar Plan was signed into law August 9, 2022 to revitalize domestic manufacturing including computer chips, create good-paying jobs and strengthen our supply chain.
This Bill was supported by 24 GOP House members and 17 GOP Senators.

PACT Act was signed into law August 10, 2022. This law expanded VA Benefits including the health issues caused from the use of Burn Pits in combat areas. This Bill was opposed by 11 Republican Senators and 174 Republican Members in the House. All Democrats supported the Bill.

The Inflation Reduction Act of 2022 (IRA), was signed into law on August 16, 2022, directs new federal spending toward reducing carbon emissions, lowering healthcare costs, increased funding for the Internal Revenue Service (IRS) to reduce tax cheating and increase tax revenue to lower the deficit. The Congressional Budget Office (CBO) estimates that the law will reduce budget deficits by $237 billion over the next decade. All GOP Senators and 207 GOP House members voted NO on this Bill despite the support by 70 % of all Voters including a majority of Republican Voters.

This is the third piece of legislation passed that seeks to improve US economic competitiveness, innovation, and industrial productivity. The Bipartisan Infrastructure Law (BIL), the CHIPS & Science Act, and IRA have partially overlapping priorities and together introduce $2 trillion in new federal spending over the next ten years.

Election Count Reform Act - Included in the 2023 government spending package was signed into law December 29, 2022. This reforms the Electoral Count Act of 1887 and clearly defines the role of the Vice President in the Congressional Certification of the Electoral Vote for President as "Purely Ceremonial".
Only 9 GOP House Members and 18 GOP Senators supported this Bill.

Respect for Marriage Act - This law codifies same-sex and interracial marriage as legal and must be recognized as valid in every state in the nation was signed into law December 13, 2022.
Just 39 GOP House Members and 12 GOP Senators supported this Bill.

These laws were enacted by Democrats with only two Bills supported by most Republicans in Congress (Juneteenth National Holliday Act & Uyghur Forced Labor Prevention Act) during the first two years of the Biden Administration. During these two years (2021 & 2022) there were 220 Democrats and 215 Republicans in the House and the Senate was split 50/50 requiring the Vice President to break any tie.

Reprinted with permission of the artist, Dale Neseman.

PAST SOCIALIST PLOTS

1844-1865 GOVERNMENT RUN POLICE AND FIRE DEPTS.

1956 FEDERAL AID HIGHWAY ACT

PUBLIC PARKS 1905

PUBLIC SCHOOLS 1790

FDR

1935 SOCIAL SECURITY

LBJ

1965 MEDICARE

NESEMAN©'21

One final thought for anyone reading this book:

Voters cannot be sure that Democrats will resolve ALL the major issues we face. However, voters can be 100% certain that Republicans will resolve NONE of our problems!

ABOUT THE AUTHOR

G ene P. Abel is a person that is not satisfied with the status quo and has always been in the forefront of change. He was born in Allentown, Pennsylvania in 1941. Mr. Abel is from a German and Scottish heritage and was educated in the public school system. He earned a B.S. from Penn State in finance/economics and an MBA from Lehigh University. He was a distinguished military graduate and received a regular army commission as a second lieutenant in the field artillery branch of the Army in 1963. Abel served as a nuclear weapons officer in Germany and a member of the nuclear release authority that begins with the President and ended with Lt Abel. Upon the completion of his tour in Germany, he spent two years as a finance officer at Ft Lewis, Washington. After four years of active duty, he accepted a reserve commission as a Captain in the Army Reserve and left active duty in 1968.

He remained in the Army Reserve until 1993 and retired at the rank of Colonel. He is a graduate of the Army War College and was awarded numerous medals including a Meritorious Service Medal on two occasions. He was promoted to Colonel after only 19 years of service and was nominated for promotion to general officer soon after completing the Army War College. However, his lack of combat service, which is most likely the result of his very sensitive assignment in nuclear weapons, prevented his promotion to the ranks of general officer. Colonel Abel's last assignment was as the Commander of the

US Army Financial Services Activity. This unit had the responsibility to the financial operations of up to 500,000 troops in time of war.

After leaving the Army, he became a financial analyst in the space and electronics industries. In 1969 he began a13 year career as a mid-level executive at the University of Pennsylvania and then at the Hahnemann Medical College and Hospital. In 1981, he was asked to return active duty to head the team redesigning the military pay system for the Army Reserve and National Guard.

On July 4, 1976, our Bicentennial, President Gerald R. Ford came to Valley Forge to sign the Law making it a National Park. At that time, Mr. Abel was the Republican Committee person from the area where Valley Forge is located and had a brief meeting with President Ford and his daughter. Mr. Abel lived on the edge of Valley Forge in an old manor house named, Willow Creek.

In 1983, upon returning to civilian life, he became an officer of a 2-billion-dollar bank where he was in charge of the bank operations at over 50 locations. In 1985, Mr. Abel returned to education and was appointed Dean of Business Services at the Reading Area Community College. His last position was the chief operating officer for one of the largest school districts in Pennsylvania. During the more than 12 years he served as the chief operating officer of the Central Bucks School District, he built over $120 million of new schools in addition to running this rapidly growing school system.

Mr. Abel was active in politics in the 70's and served as a committee person and campaign chairman for the state legislator in his area. His biography appears in Who's Who in the World and Who's Who in Finance and he was certified for Federal Senior Executive Service positions. He has written seven books and scores of articles that have been published throughout the country.

In 1998, he retired to Southwest Florida with Carol, his wife of 31 years. While living in Florida he was president of the Cape Coral Housing, Rehabilitation and Development Corporation, a nonprofit organization that provides low-income senior housing and helps

Broken Promises and Lies of the Republicans low-income homeowners repair their homes and Chairman of the Christ Lutheran School in Cape Coral, Florida. In September 2008 his wife, Carol passed away from cancer and in 2009, Mr. Abel returned to Pennsylvania. In 2010, Mr. Abel met a Jersey girl, Susan Bittner and was married in January 2011. Susan is a retired Certified Patient Care Technician at Jefferson Hospital and they live in South Jersey. Mr. Abel previously served as Church Council President at Apostles' Lutheran Church in Turnersville, NJ and remains engaged in Politics. Mr. Abel has seven children and seven grandchildren.

After retirement, Mr. Abel began to write. He has become a Best Selling Author with his Time Travel Novel, GOING BACK. His publisher, Indigo River has also launched his Romance Novel, THE INN OF DESTINY that contains a touch of the supernatural. On June 4, 2021, Indigo River will launch his non-fiction book about Extraterrestrials entitled, WHAT, IF ANYTHING, IS OUT THERE. On October 8, 2021 the sequel to GOING BACK will be released entitled, KIDNAPPERS FROM THE FUTURE.

Mr. Abel is also working on a new novel about Alien contract which will be titled, THE ALIENS STEP IN. He has created a website to keep readers informed of his writing. His website is genepabelbooks.com

Picture of Home in Valley Forge

ILT Gene Abel on 8" SP artillery Germany 1965

Me on the Howitzer

THE WHITE HOUSE
WASHINGTON

December 8, 1976

Dear Mr. Abel:

Thank you for your thoughtful letter. I certainly
appreciate your generous comments, and I was
happy to have the photos you enclosed.

While the election outcome was a disappointment,
I am deeply proud of the accomplishments of my
Administration during these past difficult years.
I am very much encouraged by our progress and
by the growing spirit of confidence in our Nation,
and I am most grateful to have had the opportunity
to serve the American people.

I send my warmest regards to you and your family.

Sincerely,

Gerald R. Ford

Mr. Gene P. Abel
Willow Creek
674 Richards Road
Wayne, Pennsylvania 19087

Letter from President Ford

SOURCES USED

American Society of Civil Engineers Brookings Institute Brown University Bureau of labor statistics

Bureau of Public Debt, Department of the Treasury Central Intelligence Agency (CIA)

Congressional Budget Office (CBO) Department of Defense (DOD) Harvard Business School

Institute on Taxation and Economic Policy (ITEP) Iraq Study Group (ISG) David Kay

National Oceanic and Atmospheric Administration (NOAA) New York Times

Office of Management and Budget (OMB)—Historical Tables Office of Personnel Management (OPM)

Organization for Economic Cooperation and Development (OECD) Philanthropy Magazine

Tax Foundation (Tax Freedom Day)

U.S. Dept. of Commerce, Bureau of Economic Analysis

INDEX

www.ingramcontent.com/pod-product-compliance
Lightning Source LLC
Chambersburg PA
CBHW032100020426
42335CB00011B/430